SPIZZERINCTUM SPEAKS OUT ON LEADERSHIP SUCCESS

SPIZZERINCTUM SPEAKS OUT ON LEADERSHIP SUCCESS

Written By: Ronald C. Butler
Communicated By: SPIZZERINCTUM

Writers Club Press
San Jose New York Lincoln Shanghai

"Leadership in the 'beautiful world of work' is all about your *relationships* with those with whom you work and socialize."

Spizzerinctum

CONTENTS

APPENDIXES & REFERENCES

FOREWORD

WHO SHOULD READ THIS BOOK?

This book is for *everyone* who is interested in achieving leadership success—college students preparing for their journey in the "beautiful world of work" and those already experiencing their journey.

Having spent thirty-three years working with college students, Ron Butler kept them in the forefront of his mind while writing this book. Ron is confident that both graduate and undergraduate students will profit immeasurably from an understanding of the leadership ideas, concepts, and principles presented in this book.

Through seminars, workshops and speeches, Ron has also shared the same leadership ideas, concepts, and principles with the personnel in a large number of profit and non-profit businesses and organizations throughout the United States. He is equally confident that the leadership ideas, concepts, and principles presented will enhance the leadership success of those who are already pursuing their careers.

Simply stated, this book is for YOU. It is all about your *leadership success* and it's importance in your life, regardless of your title, position, or job description.

DEDICATION

Ron Butler wishes to dedicate this book to the memory of William Oncken, Jr. who passed away in February 1988. Mr. Oncken and his famous Harvard Business Review article titled MANAGEMENT TIME—WHO'S GOT THE MONKEY?" and his seminar, MANAGING MANAGEMENT TIME (or GET THOSE MONKEYS ON THE PROPER BACKS) has greatly impacted Ron's leadership/management thinking and actions.

In the early 1980's, Mr. Oncken gave Ron permission to coordinate the video version of his seminar on the campus of North Carolina State University. In exchange for his generosity, Ron agreed to provide him feedback on the reactions of students, faculty, and staff which, by the way, were *always* positive. Ron doesn't remember how many times he coordinated "The Monkey Seminar," as it was often referred to, but he virtually memorized, word for word, the ideas, principles and concepts Mr. Oncken espoused.

As a presenter, Mr. Oncken was totally captivating. His great sense of humor kept his audiences laughing and attentive. His uniquely expressed ideas, concepts and principles of leadership and management brought them enlightenment and understanding. Two of his most powerful concepts are the famous "Monkey-On-The-Back" analogy and the "Molecule of Management" concept. Mr. Oncken's "Molecule of Management" concept is the most powerful concept Ron has ever learned and it is shared in this book.

One of the most memorable events of Ron's career was the day he first met Mr. Oncken. They had a wonderful lunch and as they were about to depart, Mr. Oncken gave Ron an autographed copy of his book with these words:

"Dear Ron, Please accept this, your own personal copy, as a token of my esteem. With warmest personal regards, Your friend and admirer, Bill Oncken, August, 1984"

Ron Butler is proud to honor his mentor and friend, Mr. William Oncken, Jr. by dedicating this book to his memory. Ron likens his discovery of Bill Oncken and his famous Monkey Seminar "to finding a cool mountain stream in a hot burning desert." Ron's leadership life has been positively refreshed and permanently impacted.

ACKNOWLEDGEMENTS

> Special thanks to
>
> **Sonja Beach**
>
> whose proofreading abilities
>
> and numerous suggestions
>
> helped to make this book
>
> much more readable.

Ron Butler's leadership life has been influenced by the leadership lives of many people. He constantly thinks about these special people who "touched" his life and wishes to acknowledge and thank the following:

Billie Butler, Ron's wife, and daughters, **Rhonda and Andrea** have been supportive of Ron's numerous projects throughout his 41-year career, including the writing this book. Ron loves them dearly.

Mrs. Lola Stephenson Delbridge, Ron's high school American History teacher, who literally changed his life with her expressions of confidence in his ability to achieve success and her high expectations that he would in fact do so. (Story in Chapter Seven.)

Paul Shirley, owner of Midway Grocery in Tarboro, N.C. who gave Ron his first "real job for pay" and whose words of appreciation and encouragement motivated Ron to always do a good job.

Betty Ruth & Johnny Kent, Ron's life-long and dearest friends, who taught Ron the value of helping others when they allowed him to utilize their garage to operate his three-wheel-good-humor-man-ice-cream business while he was working his way through college.

Rev. W. Harvey Morris, Ron's deceased father-in-law, whose life and character were an inspiration and role model when Ron was growing up. What a wonderful, caring, loving man!!

Mr. Joe Holliday, former Principal of Needham B. Broughton High School, who gave Ron his first two leadership jobs (World & American History Teacher and Dean of Boys) and who always made him feel a valued part of the team.

Mr. George Kahdy, former Enloe High School Principal, who hired Ron as his Assistant Principal to help open Enloe in 1962 and whose warm and friendly leadership style of dealing with people continues to be an inspiration.

Mr. Jack Stewart, deceased Dean of Student Affairs at NC State University, who expressed extraordinary confidence in Ron's ability to lead by hiring him as an Assistant Director of Admission and then promoting him twice in a short period of time to University Scheduling Officer and University Registrar.

Dr. Banks Talley, former Vice Chancellor for Student Affairs, NC State University, who said when Ron informed him that he was taking a job at Florida International University, "Go ahead, get it out of your system, I'll get you back one day." Five years later, Dr. Talley paid Ron one of the greatest compliments of his career by asking him to return to NC State as Associate Vice Chancellor for Student Affairs.

Dr. Thomas Stafford, Vice Chancellor for Student Affairs at NC State University, whose belief in Ron's leadership led him to give Ron the overall responsibilities for the Division of Student Affairs' Arts and Activities Programs. This array of responsibilities, which included the opportunity for Ron to coordinate the development of the Student Leadership Center and the Leadership Development Series, resulted in Ron having ten of the most exciting and challenging years of his career.

Leo *"MasterBuck"* Buckmaster, Jim *"BundyWorks"* Bundy, and Allen *"BradyBunch"* Brady were Ron's colleagues and close friends at NC State University. They were an inspiration to Ron as they worked together. In retirement, Ron and the 4B's stay in "email touch" on an almost daily basis. What a joy to have friends of their caliber!

Hal Burrows, co-author of THE ONE-MINUTE MANAGER MEETS THE MONKEY, who introduced Ron to William Oncken, Jr. and from whom Ron has learned a great deal about leadership and management. Occasionally, Hal and Ron team-up and co-present a leadership/management seminar.

Bill Oncken III, son of William Oncken, Jr., and special friend, who gave Ron permission to share several of his father's ideas and concepts in this book. Ron is most grateful to Bill for this special favor.

Dr. Louis Schmier, Professor of History at Valdosta State University whose books, RANDOM THOUGHTS I and II, and whose internet-accessible essays, RANDOM THOUGHTS, have greatly influenced Ron's passion for touching the lives of students and others with whom he works. Dr. Schmier created Appendix A, Spizzerinctum Jargon.

INTRODUCTION

WHO IS SPIZZERINCTUM?

Hello! My name is SPIZZERINCTUM.

I'm the new, non-gender character that has been created to visually represent the word, SPIZZERINCTUM, to all the world. Never heard the word? Don't know what I'm talking about?

Okay, I will tell you what SPIZZERINCTUM means, why I have been created to be its visual representation, and why I am qualified to speak out on

LEADERSHIP SUCCESS.

The word SPIZZERINCTUM can be found in any good unabridged dictionary. It is an exciting word, easily pronounced—Spizzer-RINK-tum—that simply means *"the will to succeed."* Your "will" is your *desire, determination, passion, yearning, urge, longing* to act in a particular way to have a particular thing.
You will find the following synonyms listed:
Vim, Vigor, Vitality, Energy & Ambition.

HOW'S YOUR SPIZZERINCTUM?

As your SPIZZERINCTUM, my goal is to make you and others *consciously aware* that your success is intimately tied to your SPIZZERINCTUM, your WILL TO SUCCEED.

As your "Will To Succeed," I reside inside you as your "Will Power" i.e., I am that "ever-present, deep fire within your very soul" that drives your determination to succeed.

I begin operating the moment you exercise your God-given "inalienable right of CHOICE." For example, when you CHOOSE to succeed in a particular endeavor, I, your SPIZZERINCTUM, become the "springboard for your choices and actions" by vigorously acting as your will/determination to succeed.

Don't ever forget: Without SPIZZERINCTUM, there is no success!

As you can readily see, I am a very important part of your very being. Without me operating as your "will to succeed," there can be no leadership success or, for that matter, success in any endeavor.

Now that you know who I am and how I operate, I invite you to come along as I share with you my views on this basic question:

What Makes For Your Leadership Success?

Success makes you feel soooo gooood!
Don't I look like I feel gooooooooood!

HOW'S YOUR SPIZZERINCTUM?

Spizzerinctum
Author, RON BUTLER

While I, **SPIZZERINCTUM**, am the one SPEAKING OUT ON LEAD-ERSHIP SUCCESS, I am doing so at the request of Ron Butler.

I have resided inside Ron as his SPIZZERINCTUM since he was born in 1933. He actually became aware of me when he was six years old. His Daddy use to say to him, "Boy, what you need is a little more SPIZZER-INCTUM—and get up and do what I told you." To Ron, SPIZZERINC-TUM meant "move quickly" or there was going to be an imminent collision with his Daddy's Spank-Spank! Ron heard this word often as he was growing up in Tarboro, N.C., which is, no doubt, the reason he has always moved so quickly.

It was not until he was a junior at East Carolina University in Greenville, N.C. that he learned the real meaning of SPIZZERINC-TUM. One day while working as a student assistant in the office of an English teacher, he spotted a huge, unabridged dictionary in the corner and immediately the word SPIZZERINCTUM popped into his mind. Ron sounded out the first part—SPIZZER—looked it up, and BINGO, there it was—SPIZZERINCTUM—with the definition: "the will to suc-ceed." Synonyms: Vim, Vigor, Vitality, Energy, and Ambition.

Ron has used the word SPIZZERINCTUM liberally ever since that momentous discovery. He immediately internalized the word and its meaning, becoming consciously aware that his SPIZZERINCTUM, residing "deep within his very soul," was his "will (determination) to succeed" and "the key" to his future Leadership Success as well as success in life in general.

Since Ron and I are "saddle pals together" in this venture of speaking out on leadership success, I want you to know a little about him.

Through his speeches, seminars, and workshops over a twenty-two year period, Ron assisted staff members in numerous business, education, government, civic, and religious organizations to understand, internalize, and put into practice the fundamental concepts, principles, and ideas that result in leadership success.

After a 41-year career in educational leadership, Ron retired in June of 1997. During his career, he held the following positions:

- 8 years in the Raleigh Public School System as a teacher, counselor, and Dean of Boys at Broughton High School and as Assistant Principal at Enloe High School

- 5 years as Director of Academic Operations and University Registrar at Florida International University, Miami, Florida

- 28 years as Assistant Director of Admissions, University Scheduling Officer, University Registrar, Associate Dean for Student Affairs, and Associate Vice Chancellor for Student Affairs at North Carolina State University

While at NC State, Ron took the lead in developing the Student Leadership Center and its major program, the Student Leadership Development Series. Through this program, each student has the opportunity to add a leadership dimension to his or her education experience while at NC State.

Ron has also played a leadership role in the community, having served five years as an elected member of the Raleigh Public Schools Board of Education and on many other boards and committees in Raleigh and Wake County. In retirement, Ron is continuing his interest in leadership by writing this book, giving speeches, conducting seminars, and consulting.

Part I

Leadership Fundamentals

SPIZZERINCTUM shares four leadership essays and stories, and answers four basic questions about leadership. An understanding of these basics will greatly enhance your leadership success.

- Essays & Stories About Leadership

- What Is Leadership?

- How Do I Lead Another Person Or Group?

- Where Does Your Leadership Take Place And With Whom?

- What Is The Basic Power You Were Born With That Permits Your Leadership Success?

CHAPTER ONE

Spizzerinctum Speaks Out Essays And Stories To Stimulate Your Leadership Appetite

In order to provide a solid framework for understanding leadership success, I wish to share four essays and stories that have come my way via Ron Butler. As you read them, know that I am building within you a fundamental understanding of leadership and an excitement about the importance of your leadership success.

ON LEADERSHIP

Leadership is an invisible strand as mysterious as it is powerful.
It pulls and bonds.
It is a catalyst that creates unity out of disorder.
Yet, it defies definition.
No combination of talents can guarantee it.
No process or training can create it where the spark does not exist.

The qualities of leadership are universal:
They are found in the poor and rich,
The humble and the proud,
The common man and the brilliant thinker.
They are qualities that suggest paradox rather than pattern,
But wherever they are found leadership makes things happen.

The most precious and intangible quality of leadership is trust, The confidence that the one who leads will act in the best interest of those who follow,
The assurance that he will serve the group without sacrificing the rights of the individual.

Leadership's imperative is a "sense of rightness,"
Knowing when to advance and when to pause,
When to criticize and when to praise,
And knowing how to encourage others to excel.
From the leader's reserves of energy and optimism, his followers draw strength.
In his determination and self-confidence, they find inspiration.

In its highest sense, leadership is integrity.
This command by conscience asserts itself more by commitment and example than by directive.
Integrity recognizes external obligations,
But it heeds the quiet voice within rather than the clamor without.

Author Unknown

I believe there is more leadership in you than you USE, than you KNOW, than you can IMAGINE. SPIZZERINCTUM

ON LEADERSHIP

The superior leader gets thing done
With very little motion.
He imparts instruction not through many words
But through a few deeds.
He keeps informed about everything
But interferes hardly at all.
He is a catalyst,
And though things wouldn't get done as well
If he weren't there,
When they succeed he takes no credit.
And because he takes no credit
Credit never leaves him.

Be still, manage things quietly,
And keep good control over everything.

In managing the affairs of men
Let rule be entrusted
To those who treat their responsibilities
As their very soul.
Leadership can be
Committed to that man
Who loves all people
As he loves himself.

As for the leader at the very top,
It is best if people barely know he exists.

Because he says very little
His words have more value;

And when the work is done,
The people are pleased,
Because they think they did it all themselves.

(From Tao-te Ching by Lao-Tzu—6th century BC)

A LEADER

I went on a search to become a leader.
I searched high and low. I spoke with authority, people
listened, but alas, there was one who was wiser than I,
and they followed him.

I sought to inspire confidence, but the crowd responded,
"Why should we trust you?"

I postured, and I assumed the look of leadership with a
countenance that glowed with confidence and pride.
But many passed me by and never noticed my air of elegance.

I ran ahead of the others, pointing the way to new heights.
I demonstrated that I knew the route to greatness.
And I looked back, and I was alone.
What shall I do? I queried. I've tried hard and used all that I know.

And I sat me down, and I pondered long.
And then I listened to the voices around me.
And I heard what the group was trying to accomplish.
I rolled up my sleeves and joined in the work.
As we worked I asked,
"Are we all together in what we want to do and how to get the job done?"

And we thought together, and we fought together,
and we struggled towards our goal.
I found myself encouraging the fainthearted.
I sought the ideas of those too shy to speak out.
I taught those who had little skill.
I praised those who worked hard.

When our task was completed, one of the groups turned to me and
said,
"This would not have been done
but for your leadership."
At first I said, "I didn't lead.
I just worked with the rest."

And then I understood!
Leadership is not a goal.
It's a way of reaching a goal.
I lead the best when I help others to go where
we've decided we want to go.
I lead best when I help others to use themselves creatively.
I lead best when I forget about myself as leader,
And focus on my group, their needs, and their goals.

To lead is to serve, to give, to achieve TOGETHER!

Kathryn E. Nelson

WOW! This essay is full of solid truths about leadership success. Read it again and get into your mind what the author says about "….when I lead best." Read it again and know that SPIZZERINCTUM believes and will prove that YOU ARE A LEADER! SPIZZERINCTUM

STORY OF A WISE MAN

I would like to tell you a story. It's about a wise man who lived long ago and very far away. This wise man was very kind and loving and was, consequently, much beloved by the people of this ancient land.

In the same land, there was a nobleman, a prince, who hated this wise man. He saw the wise man as taking from him the love of the people. The people listened to the wise man, not the prince, and that angered the prince beyond belief.

One day, the prince said to his followers, "I have a plan whereby I can discredit the wise man, a way in which I can make him appear to be a fool. Each day, the wise man goes to the market place where he speaks to the people and gives them advice. Tomorrow, when the people gather, I will go to the square disguised as a peasant. In my hand I shall hold a white dove. When the crowd has gathered, I shall raise my voice above the crowd and say, *'Wise man! I have a simple question for you. This dove which I hold in my hand—is it alive or dead?'* Now, while this appears a simple question, it is not, for if he says it is dead, I will open my hand let the bird fly away. If he says it is alive, however, I will crush the bird in my hand and let it fall dead to the ground. Either way he will appear to have made a mistake; either way it will appear that he cannot even tell the difference between a living and a dead bird; either way he will be discredited in the eyes of the people and will lose their love."

The next day came, and true to his word, the prince disguised himself as a peasant and, taking a white dove, he went to the marketplace. There he waited until the crowd had gathered and the wise man appeared. He made his way to the front of the crowd and raised his voice. "Wise man!" he shouted. "I would ask you a question. This dove which I hold in my hand, is it alive or is it dead?" The crowd grew quiet, and all eyes turned toward the wise man. The wise man paused, looked

at the prince, and said, "That which you hold in your hand. It is———-
what you make of it. It is what you make of it."

A wise answer from a wise man. Whether the dove which the prince
held was alive or dead depended upon the prince and what he did with
what he had.

Author Unknown

WOW! What a powerful story! Whether the dove that the prince
held in his hand was alive or dead depended upon the prince and what
he did with what he had. As you continue reading this book, I am asking you to figuratively hold out your hands while I share with you
many ideas, concepts, and principles about leadership success. You will
then be in the same position as the prince. While you will not have a
dove in your hands, you *will* have the ideas, concepts, and principles I
have shared, thus making the words of the wise man, "IT IS WHAT
YOU MAKE OF IT," entirely appropriate for you. Will the information
(your dove) I share remain alive to soar, grow, and flourish or will this
information about leadership success fall to the ground dead and
unused? Again, IT IS WHAT YOU MAKE OF IT. My hope is that you
will choose to allow SPIZZERINCTUM to operate as your "will to succeed," thus achieving leadership success. SPIZZERINCTUM

SPIZZERINCTUMS

Beginning with Chapter 2 and continuing throughout the remaining
chapters, you will find SPIZZERINCTUMS at the end of each chapter.
SPIZZERINCTUMS are wise sayings about leadership that will give you
helpful insights into what it takes to achieve leadership success.

The basic SPIZZERINCTUM of this book is:
LEADERSHIP SUCCESS IS SYNONYMOUS WITH ONE WORD—
SPIZZERINCTUM, "THE WILL TO SUCCEED"

Leadership lies in the "will". Your "will" is that aspect of your mind involved in choosing or deciding. Your "will" is the power you possess for controlling your actions, impulses, or emotions. Your "will" acts as an "automatic pilot" that keeps your leadership actions on course.

CHAPTER TWO

Spizzerinctum Speaks Out! What Is Leadership?

When asked to define leadership, most people can't do it. They know that they *should* know what it is and be able to communicate it intelligently without mumbling and becoming embarrassed, but they can't.

I believe leadership success requires knowing exactly what leadership is and knowing it well enough to tell someone else. After all, you really don't know something until you can communicate it intelligently to someone else. Having a good definition in mind that can be shared without consciously thinking about it is part of that knowing. Would you really like to know a good, understandable definition of leadership? Here are some excellent, meaningful definitions. I suggest that you read each of them carefully and thoughtfully, then choose the definition that most appeals to you and compare it with my favorite definition that appears later in this chapter.

- LEADERSHIP is an interaction among people that has certain effects.

- LEADERSHIP is the capacity to move, inspire, and mobilize people for a purpose.

- LEADERSHIP is the accomplishment of a goal through the directions of human assistants.

- LEADERSHIP is getting others to do what they do not want to do and like it. (Harry Truman)

- LEADERSHIP is the ability to create a vision and then to communicate that vision successfully.

- LEADERSHIP is acting on a belief and influencing others to buy into those values.

- LEADERSHIP is your ability to inspire confidence and support among the men and women upon whose competence and commitment your performance depends.

- LEADERSHIP is the process of persuasion and example by which an individual (or a leadership team) induces another person or group to take action that is in accord with the leader's purposes or the shared purposes of all.

- LEADERSHIP is the activity of influencing people to cooperate toward some goal which they come to find desirable.

- Leadership is the capacity and will to rally men and women to a common purpose, and the character which inspires confidence.

- LEADERSHIP is a serving relationship that has the effect of influencing and facilitating human relationship and human development.

- LEADERSHIP is the art of influencing others to their maximum performance to accomplish a task, objective, or project.

- Leadership is inspiring and helping others to work toward a goal.

- Leadership is the art of behaving is such as manner that you will influence (inspire) others to let nothing keep them from doing their best.

- Leadership does not mean getting others to do their jobs. It means influencing others to do their best, then the job will be done right.

While all of these definitions are excellent, each providing important, defining information about leadership, I have a favorite one-word definition that best explains the basic function of leadership. Try to determine that word by reviewing the definitions above, then choosing the word that you believe best describes the *basic function* of leadership.

LEADERSHIP is _____.

I hope you identified the word I have in mind, but in case you did not, here it is: INFLUENCE. When you stop and analyze the specific behaviors involved in leading another person or group, regardless of position or title or job responsibilities, I believe you will agree that the actions (behaviors) of one's influence best defines leadership. Therefore, my favorite definition is: **LEADERSHIP IS INFLUENCE.**

Let's take a close look at this word—INFLUENCE. The dictionary gives a number of definitions and synonyms; the ones that best fit our leadership emphasis are these:

- "a power exerted over the minds and behavior of others"
- "the act or power of producing an effect"
- "pull," "clout"

WOW! Just think—your leadership is your influence and your influence is a power you possess that effects the behavior of others.

In terms of your leadership success, think of the actions (behaviors) of your **influence** as producing the following positive results:

- Inspiring and helping people with whom you work to help you to get your job done.
- Setting an example that others will happily choose to follow.
- Helping to settle differences by encouraging cooperation.
- Introducing new ideas that help solve problems and create new opportunities.
- Interacting with others as often as possible and expressing your thoughts and feelings in a positive manner to create trusting relationships.
- Being a good communicator and listener, thus helping to avoid misunderstandings that may lead to conflict.
- Being friendly, understanding, and fair, thus helping to create a trustful working environment.
- Accepting responsibility for your actions, thus inspiring others to do the same.
- Being willing to try new ideas and new ways of doing things, thus encouraging others to become more flexible and less rigid.
- Sharing responsibilities so everyone can feel a part of the accomplishments.
- Offering help and information in order to get the job done right.
- Being decisive, energetic, and enthusiastic so others will enjoy your presence.

Just suppose for a minute or two that your influence (your behaviors) with others was such that the above results were a reality of your leadership life. WOW! No doubt about it, everyone would marvel at your leadership success.

This is the perfect moment to keep my promise of proving to you that you were born a leader. Since your leadership is your influence, and since you were born with an influence, I must conclude that you were born a leader.

Simple, but oh so profound!

Now, I did *not* say you were born an effective leader, did I? No, fortunately, there is a great deal that can be learned about leadership success, but the fact remains that you and every other person were born a leader. Because this is true, it is your responsibility to learn as much as possible about using your leadership/influence effectively as you work with people. Let's begin by reviewing and internalizing these simple, basic truths:

- **Leadership is your influence of people; therefore, leadership is the process of influencing.**

- **Your influence is expressed by the behaviors/actions of your choice.** (Chapter 11 is all about behaviors and actions.)

- **You were born with an influence; therefore, you were born a leader.**

If you are ever to be an *effective leader,* you must learn to use your influence wisely. You don't have to be especially talented, highly educated or financially wealthy to be an effective leader. However, you do have to understand other people—how they feel, what makes them tick, and how to influence them. To help you to do this is the major reason I'm **SPEAKING OUT ON LEADERSHIP SUCCESS.**

SAY YES TO LEADERSHIP SUCCESS AND SPIZZERINCTUM WILL SEE TO IT THAT LEADERSHIP SUCCESS SAYS YES TO YOU.

YOUR THOUGHTS MAY DETERMINE WHAT YOU WANT BUT YOUR SPIZZERINCTUM DETERMINES WHAT YOU GET.

LEADERSHIP SUCCESS
STARTS IN YOUR MIND WITH A CHOICE.

SPIZZ

SPIZZERINCTUMS

*(Wise sayings that will give YOU insights into
what it takes to achieve LEADERSHIP SUCCESS)*

LEADERSHIP

We need successful leaders! Potentially successful leaders are all around us—at work, at home, in the chair next to you. In fact, they may even be sitting in YOUR chair. Unknown Source

People don't want to be managed; they want to be led. Unknown Source

You manage things, but lead people. Grace Hopper

Regardless of the power associated with their job responsibilities, LEADERS don't force other people to go along with them, they INFLUENCE them along. Unknown Source

LEADERS will not experience long-term success unless a lot of people want them to. John Maxwell

The root of ineffective leadership is the corruption of the will. A.W. Tozer

The most effective leadership is by example, not edict. Unknown Source

True leadership must be for the benefit of the followers, not the enrichment of the leaders. Unknown Source

Success is generally defined as a favorable or satisfactory outcome or result. LEADERSHIP SUCCESS is having a favorable or satisfactory outcome or result with PEOPLE. SPIZZERINCTUM

A good leader is a person who takes a little more than his share of the blame and a little less than his share of the credit. Unknown Source

I have come to believe that poor performance on the part of a staff member is 80% at least the fault of the "boss". It is the LEADERS job to INFLUENCE (to coach) the staff member into a position where he/she can be successful. Unknown Source

Leadership is a privilege, and with privilege comes responsibility. Unknown Source

Real leaders are ordinary people with extraordinary determination. Unknown Source

Leadership is both something you are and something you do. Fred Smith

Good leaders must first become good servants. Robert Greenleaf

Leadership is developed, not discovered. Unknown Source

Perhaps true leadership is uncommon in today's society because it's not genuinely understood and often been misinterpreted. Donald Phillips

The successful leader is the one who makes the right move at the right moment with the right motive. Unknown Source

Leadership is leaders inducing followers to act for certain goals that represent the values and the motivations—the wants and needs, the aspirations and expectations—of both leaders and followers. And the genius of leadership lies in the manner in which leaders see and act on their own and their followers' values and motivations. James MacGregor Burns

Leadership does not mean getting people to do their job. It means getting people to do their best. Harvey Mackay

Leadership is the art of behaving in such a manner that you inspire (influence) others to do their best. Unknown Source

Leadership is not just knowing what you stand for, but what you're willing to stand up against. Harvey Mackay

Successful leaders are those who are CONSISTENT in demonstrating behaviors of their influence that put others first. Unknown Source

Leadership in the "beautiful world of work" is all about professional relationships. SPIZZERINCTUM

The best way to truly understand leadership is to learn about people and how to understand and deal with their attitudes and behaviors. Unknown Source

You can learn as much from negative leaders as positive leaders. Learning what not to do is as important as learning what to do. Unknown Source

Your job title is just a label. Your LEADERSHIP is a reputation that you must personally earn. Unknown Source

When it comes to your leadership, a *title* is not *vital*. SPIZZERINCTUM

The *will* to achieve leadership success is more important than specific skills. SPIZZERINCTUM

Leadership is all about relationships with people. SPIZZERINCTUM

Think like a LEADER, you are one! Unknown Source

Successful leaders are those who are *flexible* as they work with the people in their molecules. Spizzerinctum

Leaders are *pullers* rather than *pushers*;

Leaders are *inspirers* rather than *dictators*;

Leaders are *vision-communicators* rather than *nit-pickers*; Leaders are *enablers* rather than *hobblers*; Leaders are *challengers* rather than *drill sergeants*;

Leaders are *listeners* rather than *non-stop broadcasters*; Leaders are *lifelong learners.* Jack McCall Ph.D

CHAPTER THREE

Spizzerinctum Speaks Out! How Do You Lead Another Person Or Group?

The essence of leadership is working with and through other people. Your influence is the basic behavior/action of your leadership; therefore, leadership is nothing more or less than your influence.

If your leadership is your influence, then how do you influence people? Notice I said *people*. Your leadership (influence) always relates to people; your management always relates to things. A wise man once said, "You cannot manage people, they are unmanageable." I heartily agree—**YOU LEAD PEOPLE; YOU MANAGE THINGS!** Got it? If you understand that the actions of your leadership are always with people and that when you lead, you are using your influence with people (not things), it will help you become a more effective influencer.

By the way, please internalize this truth right now: The purpose of exerting your influence is to get and hold the support of the people with whom you work to the degree sufficient to get your job done.

The dictionary defines influence as "a **power** exerted over the minds and behavior of others." Therefore, your leadership is the power of your influence. When exerted, your influence takes the form of "cultivating relationships with others."

What is the basis of your influence, the kind of influence that will get and hold the support of the people on whom you must depend to get your job done? Bill Oncken, Jr., Ron's leadership mentor stated, "The basis of your support is the influence of your **competence, personality,** and **character** as perceived by the people with whom you work." I like to think of these traits as the components of your influence. Let me hasten to agree with Mr. Oncken who stated emphatically that it is not these traits per se, but others' experience with them over time that determines their confidence in your competence, rapport with your personality, and respect for your character. Let's take a close look at these components on your influence:

COMPETENCE: Your competence, as a source of your leadership/influence, is the degree to which others have confidence in your competence, i.e., confident that you know what you are doing and what you are talking about. Let me illustrate by asking this question: Have you ever been working with someone, perhaps your boss, and the thought passed through your mind that the boss did not know what he was doing or what he was talking about? If you have ever had this experience, you can be sure of one thing: the competency component of the boss's influence was not working as it relates to your confidence in his/her competence. What happens to your competence as a component of your influence when a person with whom you work has this same thought about your leadership?

PERSONALITY: Your personality, as a source of your leadership, is the degree to which others enjoy rapport with your personality, i.e., find you easy or difficult to listen to, to talk to, or to do business with. For example, have you ever had these thoughts about your boss: "I wish I didn't have to meet with the boss; he is so difficult to talk to, he doesn't listen, and he is extremely difficult to do business with?" If you have ever had this experience, you can be sure of one thing: the personality component of the boss's influence was not working as it relates to your rapport with his personality. What happens to your leadership when someone with whom you are working has such thoughts about you?

CHARACTER: As you cultivate the support of others, they get to know you. If they sense and experience a "basic goodness" in your actions and thinking, they will respect your character. Thus, your character, as a source of your Leadership, is the degree to which others trust your personal commitment not to allow them to wind up with the proverbial "short end of the stick" if they take you at your word. If you have respect for someone's character, it means that you trust that person. In this regard, I have some helpful thoughts about the tremendous value of trust and trusting relationships as they relate to your leadership success.

TRUST AND TRUSTING RELATIONSHIPS

- DEFINITION: Trust is the complete assurance and confidence regarding the character, ability, strength or truth of someone or something.

- SYNONYMS: Faith, Hope, and Reliance.

- RELATED WORDS: Assurance, Certainty, Belief, Sureness.

- CONTRASTING WORDS: Doubt, Skepticism, Suspicion, Uncertainty, Mistrust.

- **TRUST** is the confidence and assurance that you will do exactly what you say you will do, when you say you will do it. If you change your mind, you will let the other person know in advance so that he or she will not be harmed by your actions. If others perceive you this way, they will trust you.

- **TRUST** is a quality we extend to those who appear to offer us basic support and who seem to value our ways of contributing to the organization's effectiveness.

- The **trusting** relationship is the most efficient leadership tool ever invented. No other device saves more time or promotes more organizational effectiveness.

- The secret cement of any organization is **TRUST**. Almost anything will work when enough trust is present. Without it, nothing works.

- Who are the people you trust? You trust those (boss, co-workers, subordinates, spouse, friends, etc.) whom you believe have your best interest at heart, who are looking to recognize your strengths, who are trying to understand how you might be maximally effective, and who recognize your imperfections and areas of lesser competence but are looking to help you structure situations so your shortcomings do not become important weaknesses.

- Trusting relationships make a flawed organizational plan work, provide the key to good communication, create the conditions for teamwork, rectify badly timed actions, and soften the impact of otherwise slanderous and explosive communication. In short, our trusting relationships create the conditions for organizational and personal success.

- Nothing can erode organizational effectiveness more quickly than relationships that lack trust.

- Without trust everyday misunderstandings are taken as betrayals, simple directives become strident expressions, the best-conceived plans fail, individuals over personalize criticism and seek to hide weak spots in their performance, communication become wordy and defensive as individuals fight on issues that need to be open-mindedly discussed; and risk-taking, innovation, and creativity are stifled as individuals place "not making a mistake" ahead of seeking out new opportunities and taking chances

- Without trust there is backbiting, gossiping, running each other down, avoidance of one another, and other equally detrimental types of behaviors.

I view trust as "the cornerstone of effective human relationships." If your leadership (influence) of others is going to be successful, you must be trusted. Whose fault is it if someone does not trust you? I believe it is your fault. Why? Because whether you like it or not, you have acted/behaved in such a manner as to destroy the trust; thus, it is your responsibility to deal with people in such a manner that they will trust you. The same is true if you do not trust someone; it becomes his or her responsibility to behave in such a manner as to regain your trust. The bottom-line truth is YOU are not going to respect another person's leadership unless you trust that person. The same is true about your leadership; others must trust you if you are to be successful.

If you accept the fact that trust is vitally important, how do you develop it? The best way to develop trust is by building respect for individual differences that enables you to relate to another's interests, even if you disagree with him or her. This kind of trust can weather changes in goals or events because it's based on mutual understanding.

Remember the essay I shared earlier, entitled ON LEADERSHIP? Let's revisit the truths of that third verse:

**"The most precious and intangible quality
of leadership is trust,
The confidence that the one who leads
will act in the best interest of those who follow.
The assurance that he will serve the group
without sacrificing the rights of the individual."**

Successful leaders build trust. They do not hide their opinions and convictions and people respond favorably. People would rather follow a leader they disagree with than one who is wishy-washy and untrustworthy.

Have you ever witnessed or been involved in a situation/relationship where trust was absent? Not too pleasant is it? Trust is the common element in all relationships that work. The way we behave from day to day is largely a function of how we trust the people around us. Trust leads to respect; respect leads to loyalty.

Okay! okay, I have said more than enough about trust. How do you feel about the importance of the trust aspect of the character component of your influence? Once I asked this question to a group and a woman gave this answer: "I think it is important to follow a basic Biblical truth: consider the cost in building a tower. If you first consider the cost, you will be better equipped to make promises you can keep instead of having to back out later. This improves your ability to build trust. Also, once you give your word, it is important to do whatever you can to keep it, even if it inconveniences you. It shows the other person you hold him or her in high esteem and it is a tremendous trust builder. Trust is like banking: your deposits have to be more than your withdrawals, or else you will end up in a deficit situation. Keeping your word is 'like money in the bank.' When you keep your word, you make a deposit. When you don't, you make a withdrawal. Building trust is as simple as making more deposits than withdrawals."

How do you influence another person or group? There are three ways. These three ways are the components of your INFLUENCE. They are: Competence, Personality, and Character (Trust). Others must have *confidence* in your *competence, rapport* with your *personality*, and *respect* for your *character* in order for these components of your Influence to work for you. When exerted, these components work as the *power* of your influence to cultivate the support of those in your Molecule. SPIZZERINCTUM

SPIZZERINCTUMS

(Wise sayings that will give YOU insights into
what it takes to achieve LEADERSHIP SUCCESS)

COMPETENCE—PERSONALITY—CHARACTER

Watch your thoughts; they become words.
Watch your words; they become actions.
Watch you actions; they become habits.
Watch your habits; they become character.
Watch your CHARACTER; it becomes your DESTINY. Frank Outlaw

A trusted leader is one who shares the credit with the people who did all the work. Unknown Source

Character is what you are when no one else is around to observe your behavior. Unknown Source

Ability may get you to the top, but only character will keep you there. Unknown Source

A leader's success is related directly to the components of his/her INFLUENCE, i.e., Competence, Personality, and Character. SPIZZER-INCTUM

As a leader, your values are your most important asset. The people with whom you work will see you according to what you believe and act upon. What you believe and act upon is more important than your skills and will influence others much more readily. SPIZZERINCTUM

The best judges of your character are the people you work with. They are the ones who observe and experience your behavior almost every day. Unknown Source

To be successful, the leader must be perceived by others as competent, personable, and trustworthy. Unknown Source

Others trust of you is achieved by the many *actions* of your *influence* and lost by only one. SPIZZERINCTUM

Every man is the architect of his own character. Unknown Source

Those entrusted with leadership, whatever their field, bear a special responsibility to uphold the highest standards of moral and ethical conduct, both publicly and privately. Billy Graham

A leader's moral character, first of all, influences the way he or she does his or her job. Billy Graham

CHAPTER FOUR

Spizzerinctum Speaks Out! Where Does Your Leadership Take Place And With Whom?

Your leadership (and management activities) takes place in your **MOLECULE OF LEADERSHIP.**

The molecule concept comes from the brilliant mind of William Oncken, Jr. Ron says the molecule concept is the most powerful leadership concept he has ever learned. Therefore, it is a distinct pleasure to share Mr. Oncken's molecular ideas, concepts, and principles with you.

Your molecule consists of the people with whom you work to get your job done. These people fall into four different categories: **boss, internal peers, subordinates, and external peers.** You are the nucleus of your Molecule. Let's take a close look at its various components.

BOSS: The person to whom you are accountable for what you do in the organization.

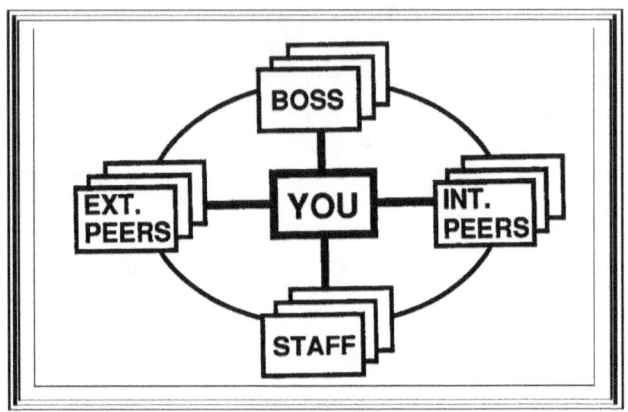

INTERNAL PEERS: The people within your organization with whom you work. These are support people. They may be in any number of departments, but their primary responsibility is to support you and others within your organization.

STAFF: The people who are directly accountable to you for what they do in the organization.

EXTERNAL PEERS: The people outside your organization with whom you work. Regardless of the people involved, the company involved or the services or products they provide, if you work with them in any manner in order to accomplish your job, they are in your molecule.

The term molecule is used because it has some illuminating analogies with a chemical molecule. Chemists define the molecule as the smallest piece into which you can divide a pure substance while maintaining all the properties of the parent substance. It looks like a monatomic molecule; there is the nucleus, things around it, and it mirrors the picture of a molecule in a general science textbook. While every molecule has the same basic elements (boss, internal/external peers, and subordinates), no one else has a molecule exactly like yours. It's going to take your leadership, your influence to get the support you need from them to be successful—but nothing says they have to support you. You have to work for their support.

The reality is, you can't get anything done at all without the active support of the people in your molecule of leadership—no person is an island. Your primary responsibility as the nucleus of your molecule is to cultivate their support. Your leadership is your action of influencing the people in your molecule. Remember: you lead *people*; you manage *things*. Therefore, getting *things* done in your molecule is a **management** action; getting *things* done through the active support of *people* is a **leadership** action. I believe that your conscious awareness of the difference between leadership and management will be helpful to you as you utilize your **SPIZZERINCTUM** to achieve leadership success.

Since it is not possible to get things done without the active support of the people in your molecule, your organization has appointed someone to see to it that you get support when you need it. Do you have any idea who has been appointed? Perhaps you are thinking the "someone" who has been appointed is someone else. Sorry to disappoint you, but **YOU** were delegated this responsibility when you were hired and first entered your molecule. Why? The reason is simple—you are the person in your molecule in the best position to handle this responsibility. No doubt about it—you are in the best position to influence the people in your molecule. Remember that your boss has a molecule with the same components of people that you have in your molecule. The same is true of your internal/external peers and subordinates. This is why I use the chemical analogy of the molecular structure—everyone's molecule has the same properties (components).

I now wish to share a very important basic responsibility you have as you work with the people in your molecule:

It should be a condition of your employment (included in your job description) that you will get and hold the active support of the people in your molecule to a degree sufficient to enable you to do the kind of job you are paid to do. You are fully and finally responsible and accountable for the kind of active support you are able to get from them.

Ever heard of the "Unit President" concept? It goes like this: "Every manager from first line supervisor through the chief executive officer is right now the president of that portion of the organization over which he has jurisdiction and shall be expected to live up to the requirements thereof."

In this connection, I wish to give you a promotion. Right now, I hereby promote you to the position of **President** of your molecule. As you pursue your career, you may never get to be the **President** of an organization or anything else, but you are right now and forevermore the **President** of your **Molecule Of Leadership**. Congratulations on your promotion! I challenge you to begin to act presidential.

Where does your leadership (and management) take place and with whom? You got it—in your molecule with your boss, internal peers, external peers, and subordinates.

My hope for you is that you will indeed experience LEADERSHIP SUCCESS as you work with the people in your MOLECULE.

SPIZZERINCTUMS

(Wise sayings that will give YOU insights into what
it takes to achieve LEADERSHIP SUCCESS)

MOLECULE RELATIONSHIPS

If you are having trouble with someone in your Molecule, try to get to know that person better—you may discover you have something in common. Unknown Source

You must view the people in your Molecule as candles that need to be lit by the power of your INFLUENCE. Unknown Source

The primary factor that determines a leader's success is his or her ability to deal with people. Unknown Source

You can get what you want, if you help the people in your molecule get what they want. SPIZZERINCTUM

It is better to have one person working *with* you than three people working *for* you. Unknown Source

He who has control of the timing and content of his job has "control" of the boss. SPIZZERINCTUM

Before criticizing your boss, take a look at both sides: your boss's side and the outside. Unknown Source

Even the Lone Ranger didn't go it alone. He had Tonto, his faithful companion. You have all those people in your Molecule. Your job is to INFLUENCE them so you can experience LEADERSHIP SUCCESS. SPIZZERINCTUM

Your leadership in the "beautiful world of work" is all about your relationships with the people in your Molecule. SPIZZERINCTUM

Treat the people in your molecule as you do your paintings— put them in the best light. SPIZZERINCTUM

CHAPTER FIVE

Spizzerinctum Speaks Out! What Is The Basic Power You Were Born With That Permits Your Leadeship Success?

You mean I was born with a power that makes leadership success possible for me? ABSOLUTELY! It has been said, "Life is 10% what happens to you and 90% how you react to it."

You were born with the inalienable right of **CHOICE**. Your right of choice is so powerful that I refer to it as your power of choice. Sadly, most people take this wonderful "power" for granted and are not consciously aware of it as they go about their daily business. My goal is to make you so consciously aware of your power of choice that you will never again take it for granted. Also, I am going to explain how this power works in relation to your leadership success as you work with the people in your molecule of leadership.

Have you ever felt that you became a victim of uncontrollable forces and circumstances and/or that you suffered in some manner because of the action of someone in your molecule? Yes, there are times when people become victims, e.g., starving children in third world countries,

Jews in Nazi concentration camps during WWII, forced robberies, and murders that occur on a daily basis, etc. However, I believe that you become a victim and suffer because of the actions of other people only when your power of choice is taken away by force. In all other circumstances and situations, you do not suffer because of the actions of other people unless you choose to allow that action to cause you to suffer. Dr. Robert Anthony even went so far as to say, "There are no victims, only volunteers."

For example, have you ever gotten your feelings hurt while working with someone in your molecule? You are never a victim of someone else's action unless you **CHOOSE** to allow that action to hurt you. Let this story explain:

Alice was attending a social gathering at her church. At one point, she met a good friend who commented that her hair looked like a "disaster zone." Alice laughed heartily and said that she had inherited the inability to fix her hair from her mother. They then went on to have a nice, friendly conversation. A few minutes later, Alice bumped into a person that she did not particularly care for. This person said virtually the same words about her hair as her good friend had said a few minutes earlier. However, this time, instead of joking about it, Alice blurted out, "Oh yeah? Yours doesn't look so hot either."

Let's analyze what happened. In the first encounter, Alice made the choice not to get her feelings hurt and joked about the comment on her hair. In the second encounter, she made the choice to have hurt feelings and to lash out with an equally uncomplimentary comment. Alice exercised her power of choice in both situations. No one can hurt your feelings without your permission. As long as you have the power of choice, you never suffer or become a victim because of someone else's actions. Some people believe that alcoholism is a disease and that those who are addicted have lost control. It may well be a disease, however, the reality is that no one is able to overcome this disease/addiction unless they make a choice to do so? Your power of choice is always with you.

You may not be able to control your boss's actions toward you, but you know something? You have a choice whether or not to work for that boss. Either way, it is your choice.

Has someone in your molecule ever said or done something that made you angry? It's rather strange when you think about it, but when someone does something you don't like, you sometimes feel it is okay to become angry. Not only do you feel it is okay to become angry, but it is okay to remain angry until he or she change their ways or apologizes. I believe, and strongly so, that it is *not* okay to become angry just because people do not live up to your expectations of them. Notwithstanding, I believe that you do have a choice of whether or not to become angry and/or to remain angry. There is no connection between the behavior of another person and your anger. It does not matter how unfairly, unjustly, or thoughtlessly someone has treated you; you become angry (and remain angry) because you make the choice to do so. The truth is you make yourself angry. Others cannot force you to become or remain angry without your permission. This is something you do to yourself. Don't we all waste a lot of time, energy, and thought when we become or remain angry over the actions of others? As long as I have the power of choice, I never suffer or become a victim because of someone else's actions.

I believe everything is a choice and every choice has an end result. If you make good choices, practically everything is possible. If you make bad choices (or choose not to make choices), eventually someone else will begin making your choices for you.

Further, I believe a person is never a failure until they **blame** someone else. As you work with the people in your molecule, one of the most counter-productive behaviors in which you can engage is blaming others. It's a lot easier sometimes to blame someone else for what may have really been your fault than to do something about your shortcomings. Who is to blame for your shortcomings? You are!

When you blame someone else for something, what you are really trying to do is avoid taking responsibility for your behavior. Blaming others usually involves making **excuses.** Dr. Leroy Walker, former Chancellor of North Carolina Central University, said the theme of his administration was "Excellence without excuses, share the responsibility." With this theme, Dr. Walker was wisely encouraging the students, faculty, and administrators of the University to achieve the excellence of which they were capable without making excuses, i.e., without blaming others.

Someone has defined an **excuse** in this manner: **"An excuse is a tool of incompetence built on monuments of nothingness and those of us who specialize in them are seldom good for anything else."** Wow! Suppose you had to write this statement one hundred times every time you made an excuse about something? How many times would it take to cure you of making excuses? If you are to ever achieve leadership success, you must avoid blaming others and making excuses. When you choose to blame another person, you surrender your power to have a good working relationship with that person.

Dr. William Glasser, author of the book *REALITY THERAPY*, once stated that healthy people do not make excuses. To drive this point home, Glasser said, "There is never a good reason to excuse yourself for being late. Let's say you've missed an appointment for any number of what you consider good reasons: traffic was heavy; the subway broke down; the elevator stalled; you took a last minute phone call." According to Glasser, you should have taken all those possibilities into account and allowed sufficient time. He added that the only pertinent **excuse** for being late is, "I'm sorry, I guess I'm incompetent to run my life." (Special note: SPIZZERINCTUM understands the tongue-in-cheek point Glasser is making about being late and not making excuses. Notwithstanding, you are encouraged not to take this illustration so literally that you believe you should always have complete control of all the circumstances in your life and that when something happens over which you have no control, it suggests you're "incompetent to run my life." Realistically, there are times when you do not have complete control over certain circumstances.)

Instead of blaming others when something is not to your liking, why not make the choice to be fully responsible and accountable for everything that happens in your molecule of leadership? To emphasize this point, consider what Samuel Hoffenstein once said, "The trouble with me is everywhere I go, I go too, and that causes me problems." Hoffenstein's statement emphasizes the point that as you work with the people in your molecule, you are involved in all that happens; therefore, the cause of a given problem may be you. True, the problem may not be your fault; however, since it happened in your molecule it is your responsibility to deal with it. Remember, if you want to achieve leadership success, it is your responsibility to cultivate the support of others; blaming them is counter-productive. Someone has observed: "The greater a person's guilt, the greater the urge to cast blame on others." Do you agree?

Blaming others is a choice—your choice—so make the right choice, do not blame others. Remember, the only time you really fail is when you blame others.

MORE ON BLAMING OTHERS

Since I really do believe that the only time you fail in your leadership role is when you blame others, I think it might be helpful to share a few additional thoughts.

Blame is a prominent behavior in many situations. It seems to be rather natural to want to blame other people, particularly, if that person is viewed as causing us a problem. But when you do, you fall into the trap of believing you are a victim of the other person's behavior.

(Remember, I believe that you become a victim of someone else's behavior only when your power of choice is taken away by force.) Let's take a quick look at two examples of blaming behaviors:

- The minute something goes wrong, some leaders begin saying aloud for all to hear, such behavioral exclamations as: **Who is to blame this time? Who goofed up? I'm going to teach whoever did this a lesson they will not soon forget! Somebody is going to pay a pretty good price for this?**

- Another example of blaming behavior is when we choose to have derogatory thought and feelings that take the form of derogatory names such as: **He's a Jerk! She's a Wimp! She's lying! He's plain stupid!**

These types of blaming behaviors, extended to those whose behaviors we find difficult to endure, do not help in any way improve your relationships with those people and is entirely counter-productive. Have you ever thought that it takes two people for one of them to be difficult, much as it takes two people to have a marriage break-up or a disagreement. Blaming others puts the full responsibility of the problem on the other person. Also, it absolves us of the responsibility of looking at ourselves and discovering how our attitudes and behaviors may relate to the problem. Sometimes, we may be responding as much to our hot button as we are to the other person's behavior.

Why is the behavior of blaming a bad choice? One good reason is—blaming others often inhibits your ability to learn what really caused the problem in a given situation. A predisposition to blame is more often than not based on a lack of understanding of what happened and the issues that gave rise to the "happening." Another reason is—blaming often prohibits you from doing anything helpful to correct the problem. After all, isn't correcting the problem and moving on the most productive action you can make?

Blaming is all about the negative behavior of condemning others. In fact, you only have to look up the word in the dictionary to see how counterproductive it is to your goal of achieving leadership success. Blame—"an expression of disapproval or reproach; a responsibility for something believed to deserve censure; deserving reproach or punishment for some act or course of action; to criticize, censure, condemn, denounce, denunciate, accuse."

Again I say, why is the behavior of blaming a bad choice? Considering what I've shared above, I can't think of any behavior that is more counterproductive to your relationships with others than blaming. You should be *cultivating the support of those in you molecule*, not blaming them for something that happened. You simply cannot get the job done by choosing blaming-type behaviors. Don't do it! In fact, your leadership success depends on your not doing it. The bottom line is this: **Blaming others is the only time we really fail and is the single worse behavior I can think of, especially as it relates to your desire to achieve leadership success.**

In his book, "Managing Mess-Ups,": Mark Eppler lists the following results of blame-placing behaviors:

- Blame never affirms, it assaults.
- Blame never restores, it wounds.
- Blame never solves, it complicates.
- Blame never unites, it separates.
- Blame never smiles, it frowns.
- Blame never builds, it destroys.

Need more be said?

MORE ON YOUR POWER OF CHOICE

Where do your choices come from? How do they operate? Your brain is the most magnificent and effective "computer" ever invented. All of your choices come from the programs stored in your computer, i.e., your brain.

Shad Helmstetter spoke brilliantly to these questions and many others in his book entitled CHOICES. Since I heartily agree with Mr. Helmstetter's views, I would like to share some of his basic thoughts with you:

"Each of us is programmed from birth with an incredible number of chemically and electrically imprinted programs in the brain that control us, effect us, drive us, and direct our behavior every single moment of our lives.

"Our programs influence and direct what we think, how we feel, and what we do day in and day out, in every area of our lives, big and small.

"Those programs tell you who we are, what we believe, what our attitudes are, and how we feel about anything and everything.

"We are programmed by our parents, our brothers and sisters, our friends, our teachers at school, and our associates at work. Even while we are very young, those same programs that we get from others begin to form the basis of our own self-talk. Then that self-talk takes over, and we begin to feed ourselves mental programs that are, for the most part, duplicates of the same kinds of programs that we receive from others.

"In time, the complete, composite picture that we have of ourselves that we carry with us is the result of the programs that we receive from others or give to ourselves.

"That is how self-esteem, as an example, is created in each of you. We learn to believe who we are, how we should look, how we act, what we reach for in life or do not reach for, and what we achieve or do not achieve. Those programs, together with the genetic programs that we were born

with, combine to make us who we are. Everything you believe about your-self today is the result of those programs."

Spizzerinctum believes your programs relate directly to your personality and create the difference in whether or not you succeed in life, especially in your desire to achieve leadership success. Your programs make the difference in your ability to:

- make a living
- obtain the education you desire
- get the job you want
- keep in good physical condition
- relate well with the people on your molecule
- keep stress in check
- have job satisfaction
- do the things you truly want to do
- express your attitude positively
- maintain happiness
- live with integrity
- be responsible for your actions, and above all
- make choices that work for YOU instead of against you.

You live your life and make your choices based on the programming you carry with you in your brain. If you want to improve how you think, how you feel, or any aspect of your behavior, you will have to change your programs.

You can greatly improve your leadership success by storing in your computer (your brain) the helpful information and advice that I have shared with you on these leadership fundamentals:

- What is leadership?

- How do you lead another person or group?

- Where does your leadership take place and with whom?

- What is the basic power you were born with that permits your leadership success?

Could you communicate the answers to these four fundamental leadership questions to another person right now? Go ahead and try. Remember, the old saying, "You don't know something if you can't tell someone else." I believe if you have a *conscious awareness* of the answers to these four questions stored in your "computer," you have a solid foundation and a great chance for leadership success. SPIZZERINCTUM

SPIZZERINCTUMS

(Wise sayings that will give YOU insights into
what it takes to achieve LEADERSHIP SUCCESS)

CHOICE

Your greatest power: the power to choose. You were not born a winner or loser, but a choosier. Unknown Source

We cannot control the "things" that happen to us, but we can control the way we face up to them—YOUR CHOICE! SPIZZERINCTUM

When weighing the faults of others, CHOOSE not to put your thumb on the scale. Unknown Source

There are two ways we can meet a difficulty: either we can alter the difficulty or we can alter ourselves to meet it. Unknown Source

You will never find time for anything. If you want time you must make it. Unknown Source

A day of worry is more exhausting than a week of work. CHOOSE not to worry! Unknown Source

Worry does not empty tomorrow of its sorrows; it empties today of its strength. Corrie Ten Boom

As you work with the people in your Molecule, you cannot control all the things that happen, but you can choose to control the way you face up to them. SPIZZERINCTUM

Those who wish to sing always find a song. Unknown Source

The choice to utilize your "*will to succeed*" automatically activates your SPIZZERINCTUM. SPIZZERINCTUM

Your organization can put you in charge and give you a title such as manager, director, supervisor, etc. But, your organization can't make you a LEADER. That's your CHOICE. SPIZZERINCTUM

There is no such thing as LEADERSHIP SUCCESS without SPIZZERINCTUM, your "*will to succeed.*" SPIZZERINCTUM

The ladder of success doesn't care who *chooses* to climb it. SPIZZERINCTUM

The dynamics involved in making your choices insures that you cannot escape from yourself or the responsibility for your decisions. Unknown Source

CHOICE has a mysterious aspect; we will never know the full outcome of any choice we make. Unknown Source

Successfully managing your POWER OF CHOICE with its many behavioral possibilities, is the essence of your LEADERSHIP SUCCESS. SPIZZERINCTUM

Each CHOICE you make is a creative, behavioral action of your influence for which you are fully responsible and accountable. Make your choices wisely. SPIZZERINCTUM

When you look in the mirror, you are looking at the problem, but remember, you are also looking at the solution. Unknown Source

People are always *blaming* their circumstances for what they are. I don't believe in circumstances. The people who get on in this world are the people who get up and look for circumstances they want and, If they can't find them, make them. George Bernard Shaw

With reference to leadership success, *complaining* and *blaming* are *loser* behaviors. SPIZZERINCTUM

One of the most important choices you can make on a day to day basis is the choice to utilize your "will to succeed" which activates ME, your SPIZZERINCTUM. Make up your mind right now to choose me and use me often. SPIZZERINCTUM

When you choose to make excuses, you are expressing a lack of faith in yourself. SPIZZERINCTUM

If you really want to do something, you'll find a way. If you don't, you'll choose to find an excuse. SPIZZERINCTUM

Resisting the chance to prove someone wrong can be difficult. It takes a great deal of maturity, not to mention foresight, to avoid blame and press on with the problem. The emotional impact of finding fault and placing blame can cause more damage than the problem itself. Unknown Source

Blame never affirms, it assaults; Blame never restores, it wounds; Blame never solves, it complicates; Blame never unites, it separates; Blame never builds, it destroys. Unknown Source

PART II

LEADERSHIP ESSENTIALS

In Part II, I share important information on six essentials and the hopes I have for your leadership success. Understanding, internalizing, and choosing to utilize these essentials will practically guarantee your leadership success.

- The Power of Your Attitude
- The Power of Your Expectations
- The Power of Your Praise
- Job Satisfaction
- Handling Change & Conflict
- Leadership Behaviors
- Summary: Hopes I Have For You And Your Leadership Success

CHAPTER SIX

Spizzerinctum Speaks Out!
The Power Of Your Attitude

What is an **attitude**? What is **personality**? There is a very close relationship.

Simply stated, your personality is the composite of the social and behavioral programs in your mind that distinguishes you as an individual. These programs contain your beliefs and feelings about anything and anybody.

Your attitude is your state of readiness and the vehicle for expressing your beliefs and feeling about anything and anybody.

My overall goal in speaking out on the power of your attitude is to help you come face to face with the important role that attitude plays in cultivating the support of the people in your molecule. Building and maintaining healthy relationships with the people you work with is the key to your leadership success.

Attitudes are caught, not taught. From whom should they be caught? You! Your first responsibility as a leader is to have and maintain a positive attitude. Your attitude makes the difference and every successful leader understands this. In fact, your attitude is so powerful that it defines for the people on your molecule who you are. **WOW!!!!!!!**

When it comes to leadership success (or lack thereof), your attitude makes the difference in whether or not you are going to be an effective or an ineffective leader. Your attitude is so powerful that it can make or break your relationships with the people in your molecule. As you already know, there are two types of attitudes: positive and negative. Each of us possesses both. Each of us chooses which will be our *primary* attitude. Which type have you chosen? It *does* indeed make a difference.

Did you know your attitude is expressed even before you utter a single word? In other words, your nonverbal communication reflects your attitude. Nonverbal communication includes your appearance, posture, eye contact, and gestures. A positive attitude acts like a magnet. It not only attracts others, but they are friendlier toward you because they sense in advance that you already like them. Your warm, friendly attitude helps those in your molecule relax and feel better about themselves and you. There is no doubt about it, your positive attitude and good relationships fit together like a hand and a glove. In fact, I'll get a little dramatic and say this: *Attitude is the single most important thing in influencing people.*

Many people downplay attitude's importance in building and maintaining good relationships. To some technical skills are more important than attitude in influencing others. As a result, they have difficulty understanding why their work, while technically correct, generates a response from others that is less than enthusiastic.

Leadership success is far more dependent on a positive attitude than on technical achievement. Of course this is not to say that technical achievement is not important and can be neglected; rather, it simply means that attitude is the glue that brings your molecule together and makes success possible.

For example, have you ever known a co-worker like Joe? He is highly skilled. He always completes his assignments rapidly and on time. His quality is the best in the department. Joe has a job that requires considerable interaction with many others in his Molecule. However, he is intolerant of those who do not deliver the same quality of work as he and is not reluctant to express his opinion. The results: no one wants to work with Joe. His boss is considering changing his work assignment because his attitude has caused many problems. Despite his technical talents, Joe is ineffective in the leadership portion of his job that requires working successfully with the people in his molecule. Yes, Joe has competence, a most important component of his influence, but he is lacking in his personality component which involves getting along well with others.

THE RELATIONSHIP BETWEEN YOUR PERSONALITY AND YOUR ATTITUDE

As I stated at the outset, there is a very close relationship between your attitude and personality. Your attitude is the vehicle for expressing your personality. Your personality is the characteristic way you behave. Your behavior comes from the programs in your mind that contain your beliefs and feelings about anything and anybody—your looks, the people on your molecule, the weather, the car you drive, your job satisfaction, a mistake you made, etc. The way others perceive your personality is the key to whether or not they have rapport with your personality.

Every person is born with a basic personality structure that most likely will not change; notwithstanding, changes in behavior are quite possible. I believe you can change your behavior, but not your basic personality. Even so, the changes you choose to make in your behavior still filter through your basic personality structure.

Are you communicating your personality, the way you think and feel, with a positive attitude or a negative attitude to those in your molecule?

A positive attitude can enhance your personality traits; on the other hand, a negative attitude can diminish your personality traits. When you are optimistic and anticipate successful encounters with others, you transmit a positive attitude and the people on your molecule usually respond favorably, making your LEADERSHIP effective. When you are pessimistic and expect the worse, your attitude is most often negative and people with whom you work tend to avoid you, making your leadership ineffective.

In one sense, your attitude is nothing more than the sum total of all the daily choices (small and large) you choose to express about how you feel and think about anything. Yes, your attitude is a choice and it is your most precious possession.

A good example of a positive attitude is contained in a story that Zig Ziglar shared in one of his seminars: Zig had just come from a series of seminars. When his wife picked him up at the airport, she took their daughter Susan and her friend along for the ride. As Zig shared his excitement about the seminars with his wife, he overheard the following conversation from the back seat.

"What does your Daddy do?"

Zig's ten-year old daughter replied, "Oh, that positive thinking stuff."

Pause—"What is positive thinking?"

Another pause—"Oh, you know, that's what makes you feel good, even when you feel real bad."

If a ten-year old knows that positive thinking (transmitted by our attitudes) can change the way we feel by improving our feelings, why is it so few leaders choose not to use it in their daily relationships with the people with whom they work and socialize?

A positive attitude is the most powerful personality characteristic you can possess and, believe me, it is deeply appreciated by everyone in your molecule. You are either a positive influencer (leader) OR a negative one. There is no way to be neutral. Building good relationships in your molecule is enhanced significantly by a positive attitude. This little story illustrates both a positive attitude and job satisfaction:

There were three men digging a ditch.

A bystander asked the first ditch digger what he was doing.

The answer was, "I'm digging a ditch."

The same question was asked of the second ditch digger.

The answer, "I'm making a living."

When the same question was asked the third ditch digger, an entirely different answer came forth.

"Mister, I'm helping to build a cathedral."

Are you helping your organization build itself? If so, your attitude has already revealed such; if not, it has already revealed such!

RELATIONSHIPS

I have mentioned the word relationship numerous times. A relationship is based on the psychological feelings between two or more people. Because you can't see or touch a relationship, some people think only of the personality involved. They ignore the relationship itself. As a result, individuals often lose their objectivity. Instead of taking actions to improve the relationship, they get "persnickety" about an individual's personality as expressed by their attitude and some kind of conflict develops. Successful leaders are able to deal with the relationship issues first; thus, they are more apt to accept differences within another's personality.

However, some people would rather find new relationships than repair old ones; thus, they are never as successful in their leadership roles as they could be. In the workplace, this can mean creating factions among people and switching jobs frequently. Those who want more from their careers recognize the importance of maintaining positive relationships. When a repair job is necessary, smart leaders hasten to set things straight. They take action whether or not they are the cause of the problem. Their attitude is that the relationship is more important than the incident that caused the damage.

Working relationships, like other types of relationships, are fragile and require constant care. Once neglected, it is difficult for them to return to their previously healthy state. Positive attitudes help everyone!

Life is more meaningful, problems are far more easy to handle, goals are more attainable, mistakes less stressful, and the "beautiful world of work" is a lot more fun when you choose to maintain a positive attitude. Negative attitudes get you nothing and nowhere!

Not only your leadership success, but also the very quality of your life depends on your attitude toward yourself and toward others. Because of the great power of choice you were born with, you are the only one who can change or control your attitude. Therefore, if you want to achieve leadership success, make a choice to have a positive attitude! I know it's not easy to change your attitude and it does take time and a determined effort. Notwithstanding, the leadership success and satisfaction you experience when you act instead of react, when you see opportunities instead of problems, paves the way for LEADERSHIP SUCCESS. I like what Ann Turnage said, "Attitude is your paintbrush; it colors every situation." WOW! Is not that statement powerful and true? You better believe it!!!!!!

SPIZZERINCTUM'S ATTITUDE DETERMINATION SCALE

SPIZZERINCTUM urges you to take advantage of this opportunity to become more consciously aware of your attitude as viewed by yourself and the people in your molecule. (Remember, your attitude is your vehicle for expressing your personality, i.e., your beliefs and feelings about people and things.) Each statement below asks you to rate how you think others perceive your attitude by circling the number that best fits you. If you circle a 10, you are indicating that your attitude is positive. If you circle a 1, you are saying negative. SPIZZERINCTUM urges you to be honest.

	High (Positive)	Low (Negative)

1. Today, I believe my boss
   would rate my attitude as a.............10 9 8 7 6 5 4 3 2 1

2. Today, I believe the majority
   of my Internal Peers would
   rate my attitude as a ....…......10 9 8 7 6 5 4 3 2 1

3. Today, I believe the majority
   of my subordinates would
   rate my attitude as a.....................10 9 8 7 6 5 4 3 2 1

4. Today, I believe the majority
   of my External Peers would
   rate my attitude as a ....…......10 9 8 7 6 5 4 3 2 1

5. I believe my family would
   rate my attitude as a ....…..10 9 8 7 6 5 4 3 2 1

6. I believe most of my friends
   would rate my attitude
   as a........................…..................…..10 9 8 7 6 5 4 3 2 1

7. I would rate my attitude
   as a.........................…..….............10 9 8 7 6 5 4 3 2 1

SUMMARY QUESTIONS:

- From the results above, I believe my attitude is serving me:

  ___Very Well   ___Well   ___Not Very Well

- As Leader and President of my Molecule, I believe I need to work on changing my current behavior in order that I may develop a more positive attitude. ____Yes ____No

- ____I agree ____I do not agree with this statement: My attitude is a choice and is my most precious possession when it comes to influencing the people in my molecule.

  I hope you have a good attitude. Oh, so essential! SPIZZERINCTUM

SPIZZERINCTUMS

*(Wise sayings that will give YOU insights into
what it takes to achieve LEADERSHIP SUCCESS)*

ATTITUDE

Attitude is your paintbrush; it colors every situation. Ann Turnage
Whatever your job responsibilities—your leadership success depends on your attitude. Unknown Source
A positive attitude at work will make your daily routine more rewarding and enjoyable. Unknown Source

Your attitude is known even before you utter a single word. Unknown Source

Your attitude is not the main thing in influencing people. It is the most important thing. Unknown Source

Your attitude is the vehicle for expressing the way you feel and think about things and people. Unknown Source

A happy person is not a person in a certain set of circumstances, but rather a person with a certain set of attitudes. Unknown Source

The first responsibility of any leader is to maintain his/her positive attitude. Attitude makes the difference and every effective leader understands this. Unknown Source

You can change things if you just change your attitude. Unknown Source

There is little difference in people, but that little difference makes a big difference. The little difference is attitude. The big difference is whether it is positive or negative. Clement Stone

I have had a long, long life full of troubles, but there is one curious fact about them—nine-tenths of them never happened. Andrew Carnegie

The world is moving so fast these days that the man who says it can't be done is generally interrupted by someone doing it. Elbert Hubbard

I'm glad I am an optimist. The pessimist is half-licked before he starts. Thomas A. Buckner

You cannot climb uphill to the mountain of leadership success by thinking downhill thoughts. Likewise, you cannot achieve leadership success without **SPIZZERINCTUM**. SPIZZERINCTUM

Nowhere is a positive attitude more appreciated than in your mole-cule by the people with whom you work daily. SPIZZERINCTUM

Your smile is one expression that instantly communicates in a posi-tive manner. Unknown Source

We burn up to three times more energy being upset than being relaxed. Working three hours with a bad attitude is the equivalent of working nine hours with a good attitude. Unknown Source

Your self-image is communicated or projected to others through your attitude. Unknown Source

Your attitude is a powerful tool that can be used effectively to influence the people on your molecule. Spizzerinctum

You can call yourself an OPTIMIST if you think the E on your gas gauge stands for *Enough*. Unknown Source

CHAPTER SEVEN

Spizzerinctum Speaks Out!
The Power Of Your Expectations

One of the most powerful tools for influencing the performance of others is your own expectation. This is another power you were born with.

Psychologists have demonstrated that the power of one's expectations alone can influence the behavior of others. This phenomenon is often referred to as the Self-Fulfilling Prophecy or the Pgymalion Effect. It tells us that if we have high expectations of others (those in your molecule), they will generally live up to those expectations. Of course, the opposite is also true; if we have low expectations of their performance, they will probably meet those expectations as well.

Dr. Robert K. Merton of Columbia University first introduced the ideas of the Self-Fulfilling Prophecy in 1948. Since then, a great deal of research has been done to test Merton's theory. Dr. Robert Rosenthal performed over 400 experiments to prove that the Pygmalion Effect can significantly influence the behavior of those with whom we work and socialize.

This is not a new concept. The original Pygmalion was a prince and sculptor in Greek and Roman mythology who carved a statue of the ideal woman out of ivory. Her name was Galatea. The creation was so beautiful and lifelike that the prince fell in love with the statue. His love for the statue was so strong that he began to believe and expect that it was real. He prayed to the goddess Venus to bring Galatea to life. His prayer was granted. The statue came to life.

George Bernard Shaw's famous play **"PYGMALION"** and the musical **"MY FAIR LADY"** have a similar theme—the belief that one person by determined effort can influence the behavior of another person.

Our expectations of people and/or events are often reflected in our behavior. Once an expectation is set, even if it is not accurate, we tend to act in ways that are consistent with that expectation, and **BINGO!** The result of the expectation comes true.

According to Len Sandler's **"TRAINING"** magazine article, "Self-Fulfilling Prophecy: Better Management By Magic," the bottom line is this: "Consciously or not, we tip people off as to what our expectations are. We exhibit thousands of cues, some as subtle as the tilting of heads, the raising of eyebrows or the dilation of nostrils, but most are much more obvious and people notice those cues. The concept of the self-fulfilling prophecy can be summarized in five key principles:

- We form certain expectations of people or events.
- We communicate those expectations with various cues.
- People tend to respond to these cues by adjusting their behavior to match them.
- The result is that the original expectations become true.
- This creates a circle of self-fulfilling prophecies."

For a very simple but powerful example of how the power of expectation works, I wish to share what happened when Ron Butler's eleventh grade American History teacher, Miss Lola Stephenson, expressed her **expectation** of him.

On one occasion, early in Ron's junior year, Miss Stephenson said that she thought he would be "great" in a certain role in that year's Junior Play. She encouraged him to try out for the part. Although Ron had never been in a full-fledged play, he felt so complimented and challenged by Miss Stephenson's invitation to try out that he just could not disappoint her. He tried out for the part, won it, and had a most rewarding experience—an experience that literally changed his life by giving him the confidence that he could become "somebody". Up to that time in his life, Ron had never given a single thought to attending college, thinking that college was for others. However, on another occasion shortly after the Junior Play, Miss Stephenson asked Ron where he was going to attend college, implying that she clearly expected that Ron was planning to attend college. She suggested that he look at her college newspaper. After reading several of them over a period of weeks, Ron became very excited about college. He shocked his parents by announcing to them that upon graduation from high school he was going to attend East Carolina College in Greenville, North Carolina, only 27 miles from his home. Ron chose to become a teacher. Guess what he majored in? Social Studies! When he began his high school teaching career, guess which Social Studies course he taught? American History!

Does the Pygmalion Effect really work? You bet it does! When you make others in your molecule feel good about themselves and their contributions to the cause with your high expectations of them, you are cultivating their support and stimulating their desire to do their best.

Your expectation of others is derived from your power of choice. When expressed, your expectation becomes your influence, which, as you know, is your leadership. Believe me, there is power in your expectations of others, a valuable behavior for influencing (leading) the people in your molecule.

The power of your expectations can assist you greatly in achieving leadership success. Do you agree? To assist you in further thinking about the impact of your expectations, please give these questions some thought:

1. Who are the people in your life—in your Molecule, in your family, in elementary/high school, in college, and in your community/church—who believed in you and challenged you with their expectations to believe in yourself and reach higher than you once thought possible? Write down their names and send them a letter of thanks for touching your life.

2. What are some specific behaviors (techniques, skills, activities, communications, etc.) that will transmit your expectations to others? Write down as many as you can think of.

3. Can you think of a positive example of the Pygmalion Effect that you have observed or experienced personally? Write it down and consciously think about the dynamics involved.

4. Think of someone in your molecule and write down the specific things you can do to positively influence (transform) that person through the power of your expectations.

5. Just for fun, think about yourself as president of your molecule. Are there those in your molecule who would like to see the president "transformed" by the Pygmalion Effect? If so, since you now know how it works and how powerful it is, go ahead and tell them how to "transform" you by the power of their expectations of you. Ha! The Pygmalion Effect works both ways.

I have a question for you. Could you explain to another person, in your own words, the value and power of one's EXPECTATIONS? Go ahead and mentally give it a try. It will help cement this valuable leadership essential in your mind. Now, enjoy the following SPIZZERINCTUMS that deal with expectations. SPIZZERINCTUM

SPIZZERINCTUMS

(Wise sayings that will give YOU insights into what ittakes to achieve LEADERSHIP SUCCESS)

EXPECTATIONS

Our expectations of people and/or events are often reflected in our attitude and behavior. Once an expectation is set in our mind, we tend to act in ways that are consistent with that expectation, and the result of the expectation comes true. Unknown Source

If you have high expectations of the people in your Molecule and express them in a positive manner, the people involved will generally live up to those expectations. SPIZZERINCTUM

Consciously or unconsciously, you always get what you expect. Dr. Robert Anthony

Your expectations of others are a choice; when expressed, your expectations become your influence. SPIZZERINCTUM

Our study of effective leaders strongly suggested that a key factor was what we're calling the positive self-regard. Positive self-regard seems to exert its force by creating in others a sense of confidence and high expectations not very different from the fabled Pygmalion Effect. Warren Bennis and Burt Nunus

Whether you believe you'll succeed or not, you're right. Unknown Source

CHAPTER EIGHT

Spizzerinctum Speaks Out! The Power Of Your Praise

Another powerful tool for influencing the performance of others is **PRAISE**. Praise others for doing a good job and you will witness the power of its effects. Praise is one of the most effective ways to cultivate the support of the people in your molecule.

Research has proven repeatedly that praise works far better than criticism in getting people to do a better job. When praised, nine out of ten did a better job the next time. When criticized, only three out of ten did a better job the next time.

One of the most dominant needs of human beings is to *feel important*. This being true, what should you do as you work with the people in your molecule? It's very simple—if people need to feel they are important, and we all do, it's your job to make them feel important.

How, you ask? Read on, as I am going to share with you some of the dynamics involved in making the people with whom you work feel important. I hope you will be convinced that you have the power to praise deep within you and that this power can be easily exercised if you choose to use your power of choice.

Remember the movie monster Frankenstein? He was not even human, yet when a few kind words of praise were extended, he smiled for the first time since his creation by man. Do animals respond to kind words of praise? You bet they do, even those who live in the wild.

Well then, if praise is so powerful and effective, even with non-humans and animals, and if all of us have the ability to praise others if we choose to do so, why don't we choose to use praise more often? Of course, there are many reasons why we don't, but I'm going to concentrate on what I believe is the main reason and then give you four often-used excuses why we don't.

The main reason we don't use the power of praise more often is that we have not been programmed to so. (Remember the thoughts of Shad Helmstetter , shared in Chapter 5, who related the details of how we are programmed by our parents, brothers and sisters, our friends, our teachers at school, our associates at work, and ourselves, etc. You might find it helpful to review this information.)

How can you praise others for their achievements if your computer (mind) has not been programmed in this manner? To utilize your power of praise, you must have a "praise program" in your computer (mind) and it must be working in auto-mode, i.e., the moment you realize praise is needed, you give it—sort of like instantly checking your spelling and grammar when you are composing a document on the computer.

How do you program/re-program your computer (mind) so that praise comes naturally? Talk to yourself. Keep on telling yourself how important it is to *praise* others. Soon it will come as natural as breathing.

There are four primary excuses (not reasons) why people don't use their power of praise more freely:

Excuse # 1: WHO PRAISES ME? Leaders who don't receive praise for their efforts often feel justified in not giving praise to others.

Excuse # 2: PEOPLE WILL MISUNDERSTAND MY INTENT! Some leaders feel their attempts to praise will be viewed as insincere or manipulative—that others will think, "What does he/she want from me now?"

Excuse # 3: PEOPLE MAY TAKE THE PRAISE I GIVE THEM TO MEAN MORE THAN I HAD INTENTED. Some leaders fear that if they praise others for doing a good job, they will go away thinking everything they are doing in okay.

Excuse #4: IT'S JUST NOT MY STYLE! A surprising number of leaders avoid praising others because they think they'll be perceived as being weak or soft.

Excuses! Excuses! Excuses! You remember what an excuse is, don't you? In case you've forgotten, here it is again: "An excuse is a tool of incompetence built on monuments of nothingness and those of us who specialize in them are seldom good for anything else." The real truth is if you really want to do something, you'll find a way; if you don't, you'll find an excuse.

What have I said previously about excuses and blaming? Making excuses for your behavior and blaming others is the most counter-productive behavior you can exhibit as you try to positively influence the behavior of the people in your molecule. Just choose not to excuse and blame! Research has shown that most successful leaders PRAISE others as often as possible—not too much, not too little—but as often as possible. They have learned that there is a close relationship between the amount of praise they give others and the positive benefits they experience in return. Please note that praise is not only for those who report to you (subordinates), but for everyone in your molecule—boss, internal peers, and external peers.

Most, if not all, people in your molecule need to have their efforts and accomplishments praised with well-timed, sincere praise for something specific. It fires them up and their SPIZZERINCTUM—Vim, Vigor, and Vitality—becomes readily apparent.

Consider the specificity of this example. On one occasion, Ron Butler expressed his praise to his boss with a note that contained these words: "Wow! The suggestion you made at our meeting this morning was great! One gold star for your most creative idea! All of us left the meeting with feelings of great hope for the future. Thanks for your leadership."

If you want to achieve leadership success, take notice of your Boss doing something right and praise him/her. The same goes for the "others" in your molecule. Suppose you went up to your Boss several times a week and said, "Boss, I tell my wife/husband every night how lucky I am to be working with a person like you." If your praise is that non-specific and occurs that often, it is time "to roll up the pants because it's too late to save the shoes." This type of praise would most likely be interpreted as being too general and not very sincere—because it is not specific enough. If you express your praise sincerely, it will not get misread. BE SPECIFIC.

It is said of Thomas Jefferson that he had the gift of making others feel important, and he did so. Even those who had doubts about him, who disliked and opposed him on occasions, became his friends. Mrs. Samuel Harrison Smith gave an example of how he accomplished this. "He gave everyone an opportunity of talking," she said. "I recollect at one dinner there was a man who was silent and neglected. To him the President said, 'We are indebted to you, Mr. Collins. No one deserves more gratitude of the country.' He then described a contribution Mr. Collins had made. Every eye turned to the guest, who honestly looked more astonished than anyone else in the room. He had been a mere cipher before. Now he had become a person of importance."

Some people never realize the importance of making the people with whom they work feel important. Arline Elliott, the owner of a women's wear store said, "A good way of making a person feel like a VIP, a very important person, is to build up the value of her work. Tell her how essential her job is to your organization and how important she is to you." I heartily agree with Ms. Elliott. Most people need to feel that their contributions are important and appreciated.

Another way of making others feel important is to keep them well informed. Let them know ahead of time, if possible, when changes are about to occur. Knowing what is going to happen before it happens makes them feel important.

Offering a sincere word of praise is such a simple thing to do and one that you can do every day as you relate to the people in your molecule. You work with and meet people daily who are starving for attention, yearning to feel worthwhile about themselves and their contributions. Give them a word of praise and you will see immediately the powerful results. Here are a few ideas and thoughts on how to praise a person:

- Use words and phrases that are natural for you, such as "Good job, Phyllis!" "Excellent work Johnny." "Thanks for doing such a wonderful job, Sally." "I enjoy working on projects with you, Jackson; you are so thorough."

- Of course, there are many other ways to praise people. It may be appropriate on occasions to write a note or letter or to express your praise at evaluation time. The bottom line is do it and be sincere when you do it.

- And, remember, the people in your molecule will relate more readily to your words of praise and efforts to make them feel important when you use your natural style of communication.

The POWER OF PRAISE

is a

POWERFUL ESSENTIAL

as you strive for

LEADERSHIP SUCCESS.

SPIZZERINCTUMS

(Wise sayings that will give YOU insights into
what it takes to achieve LEADERSHIP SUCCESS)

PRAISE

A university study concluded public praise improves the performance of 90% of the population. Conversely, only 30% of those criticized in public did better in the future. James K. Van Fleet

I can live two months on a good compliment. Mark Twain

Praise Me! Recognize Me! Make Me feel my contributions are important. Rewarded behavior is repeated. Unknown Source

Except for a rare few, there are no magic words to express praise. How you say it is what makes what you say work magic for you with others. James K. Van Fleet

Twice I did well and that I heard never. Once I did bad and that I heard forever. Unknown Source

Things that get recognized and rewarded get done. Unknown Source

Too often we underestimate the power of a touch, a smile, a kind word, a listening ear, an honest compliment, or the smallest act of caring, all of which have the potential to turn a life around. Leo Buscaglia

The human spirit craves recognition. No reward compares with the power of verbal recognition. Unknown Source

A word of kindness or a word of praise is seldom spoken in vain. It is treasured by the recipient for life. Unknown Source

People don't care how much you know until they know how much you care. John Maxwell

Learn to look for the good and praise it. We must praise ourselves and each other. Unknown Source

Praise does wonders for the sense of hearing. Unknown Source

Imagine that everyone in your Molecule has a sign hanging around his/her neck that reads; "MAKE ME FEEL IMPORTANT!" Unknown Source

Nothing will improve a person's hearing more than a word of praise. Harvey Mackay

What happens to a person's SPIZZERINCTUM when they hear words like these? "You did a terrific job." "I'm proud of what you did." "I apologize, I was wrong." Unknown Source

Most people want to do a good job—as long as someone appreciates their efforts and encourages them. Successful leaders act in a variety of ways to show others that their work is valued and appreciated. Unknown Source

Even the tone and volume of your voice is a behavior of your INFLUENCE. If I raise my voice may it be only to utter words of PRAISE. Unknown Source

Exercise: There is no exercise better for your leadership heart than reaching down and lifting people up. Unknown Source

The people in your molecule have at least three *desires:* To be treated with respect and dignity; to be acknowledged and appreciated; and, to know that their work contributes to the goals and objectives of their organization. What can you do to help fulfill their *desires*? ACTIONS OF PRAISE! SPIZZERINCTUM

Praise expresses your approval of what others do. It uplifts them and inspires them to do even better. Unknown Source

When you show appreciation for what others do, you give value and validate their efforts. Unknown Source

An effective leader is just about always full of praise. Unknown Source

When dealing with people in your Molecule, make sure you don't project this message through your attitude or words,i.e. "First, let's get this straight—I am important, you are not." SPIZZERINCTUM

CHAPTER NINE

Spizzerinctum Speaks Out!
Job Satisfaction

Welcome to the "beautiful world of job satisfaction! What was that? Oh no! You say you don't have JOB SATISFACTION, but wish you did? You can! You should! And, if you desire to experience leadership success, You must!

I believe with every fiber of spizzerinctumous being that job satisfaction is not only a possibility, but a responsibility of every president of every molecule!

As we now take a brief look at another important leadership essential—JOB SATISFACTION—I invite you to keep in the forefront of your mind your power of choice. Yes, job satisfaction is a choice.

I believe it is possible for everyone to have basic job satisfaction even though some studies suggest that as many as 60% of working people literally hate their jobs.

Why is job satisfaction so elusive and difficult to achieve for most people? I believe one of the reasons is that so many people at all levels have "mentally retired." This state of mind is truly a tragedy and occurs without regard to age. A wise man once said, "The tragedy of life is not in the fact of death itself. The tragedy of life is what dies inside a man or woman while they live."

Those who have "mentally retired" have lost their SPIZZERINCTUM and are not looking for new challenges, are not interested in changing and learning new things, or doing things different or better. In fact, what a large number of job dissatisfied people are looking for these days is "less to do, more time to do it, and higher pay for not doing what they should have done in the first place."

The bottom line truth is that "mentally-retired, job-dissatisfied" people are coasting; they are going in the only direction that coasting leads—downhill. Sadly, when growth stops, decay begins. Instead of viewing their jobs as a "cool mountain stream in a hot burning desert," they think of them as a "hot burning desert—without any life-giving water."

Do you have basic job satisfaction, i.e., do you enjoy your job responsibilities and the people with whom you work? Is it a delight to go to work and help accomplish the goals and objectives of your organization? If not, you will never experience basic job satisfaction; therefore, you will never experience genuine leadership success. I have never met a successful leader who was dissatisfied with his or her job.

By basic job satisfaction, I do not mean that you never experience problems with things and/or with the people in your Molecule. We all experience problems. This is natural. We are human beings and nothing is perfect all the time. Notwithstanding, it is your responsibility to use the components of your influence (competence, personality, character) with the determination that problems will be solved, not intensified.

Why is job satisfaction so essential to your leadership success? If you do not have job satisfaction, regardless of the reason (s), your dissatisfaction becomes a part of your thinking and beliefs and is expressed by your attitude. And, as we have already learned, a negative attitude reduces your ability to positively influence the people in your molecule.

Therefore, it is most important that you choose to have job satisfaction. Remember that job satisfaction is a choice!

Let SPIZZERINCTUM tell you the story of Ron Butler's experience with job satisfaction. (As you know, ole SPIZZ has been right there inside Ron all these years, serving as his "will to succeed.")

On one occasion, Ron spoke to a large group of North Carolina State University employees at the annual Employees' Awards Luncheon. Ron chose as his subject job satisfaction and opened his talk with these words:

"I have reached a point in my life and career that finds me more excited about my job and the people I work with than at any other time I can remember. I look forward to coming to work at the university every single day. In fact, and many of you will find this hard to believe, I have never been to work a day in the past 38 years when the thought passed through my mind, 'I wish I didn't have to go to work today.' I love my work and thoroughly delight in contributing to the success of the goals and objectives of the Arts and Activities Program at NC State. I respect and enjoy the people with whom I work. I can never remember a time in my career when I did not have job satisfaction. You can too!"

Yes, you too, can experience job satisfaction. Remember the words, shared earlier, of the third ditch digger when asked the question, "What are you doing?" He looked up with a smile on his face and said, "Mister, I'm helping to build a cathedral. Helping to "build" your organization and knowing that your contributions are appreciated will bring about a sense of self-worth that inevitably leads to job satisfaction.

George Moore wrote a novel in which he told of some Irish peasants in the period of the Great Depression. In an attempt to provide work for the men who had lost their jobs, the government put them to work building roads. At first, the effort appeared to be successful. The men worked well and sang their Irish songs until they discovered that the roads they were building had no destination, but led to a dead end and stopped. The men suddenly realized that the only meaning in their work was that it provided employment. It was not enough! The men quit their work and stopped their singing. Explains the author: "The roads to nowhere are difficult to make. For a man to work well and sing, there must be an end in view."

If this story teaches us anything, it is this: In order to have job satisfaction, "there must be an end in view." In other words, your work must be meaningful and provide you with a sense of satisfaction so you can "sing." Since you are the President of your Molecule and, therefore fully responsible and accountable for everything that happens, you should choose not to work another day without job satisfaction. As you have already learned, you have the power of choice to do it—so why not choose to do it.

In keeping with the thought of what you must do to achieve job satisfaction, let me share this powerful essay. As you read it, ask yourself what would happen to a person's job dissatisfaction if the advice given was internalized and implemented.

THE STATION
By Robert Hastings

"*Tucked away in our subconscious minds is an idyllic vision. We see ourselves on a long, long trip that almost spans the continent.*

"*We are traveling by passenger train, and out the windows we drink in the passing scene*
- *of cars on nearby highways,*
- *of children waving at a crossing,*
- *of cattle grazing on a distant hillside,*
- *of smoke pouring from a power plant,*
- *of row upon row of corn and wheat,*
- *of flatlands and valleys,*
- *of mountains and rolling hillsides,*

- *of city skylines and village halls,*
- *of biting winter and blazing summer and cavorting spring and docile fall.*

"But uppermost in our minds is the final destination. On a certain day at a certain hour, we will pull into the Station. There will be bands playing and flags waving. Once we get there, so many wonderful dreams will come true. So many wishes will be fulfilled and so many pieces of our lives finally will be neatly fitted together like a completed jigsaw puzzle. How restlessly we pace the aisles, damning the minutes for loitering—waiting, waiting, waiting for the Station.

"When we reach the station, that will be IT! we cry. Translated IT means:

- When I'm 18, that will be IT!
- When I buy a new 450 SL Mercedes Benz, that will be IT!
- When I put the last kid through college, that will be IT!
- When I have paid off the mortgage, that will be IT!
- When I get a promotion, that will be IT!
- When I reach the age of retirement, that will be IT! I shall live happily ever after.

Unfortunately, once we get the IT, the IT disappears. **The Station** somehow hides itself at the end of the endless track.

Sooner or later, we must realize there is no station, no one place to arrive once and for all. The true joy of life is the trip. The station is only a dream. It constantly outdistances us.

"Relish the moment" is a good motto, especially when coupled with Psalm 118:24: "This is the day the Lord hath made; we will rejoice and be glad in it."

It isn't the burden of the today that drives men mad, rather it is regret over yesterday or fear of tomorrow. Regret and fear are twin thieves who would rob us of today.

So, stop pacing the aisles and counting the miles. Instead,

- *climb more mountains,*

- *eat more ice cream,*

- *go barefoot more often,*

- *swim more rivers,*

- *watch more sunsets,*

- *laugh more, cry less.*

*Life must be lived as we go along. **The Station** will come soon.*

Wow!!! Isn't THE STATION powerful? Take a moment and think about these truths:
- "Life must be lived as we go along."
- "We must realize there is no station, no one place to arrive once and for all."
- "The true joy of life is the trip."
- "This is the day the Lord hath made; we will rejoice and be glad in it."
- "The station is only a dream. It constantly outdistances us."
- "So stop pacing the aisles and counting the miles. Instead, climb more mountains, eat more ice cream, go barefoot more often, swim more rivers, watch more sunsets, laugh more, cry less."
- "Life must be lived as we go along. The Station will come soon."

If you are sincere in wanting to experience job satisfaction, just internalize the meaning of these powerful truths contained in "THE STATION." Talk to yourself until these truths are happily living in your mind where they will become a part of your personality and be transmitted by your attitude for all the world to see that you have achieved job satisfaction. *CONGRATULATIONS!!!* SPIZZERINCTUM

SPIZZERINCTUMS

(Wise sayings that will give YOU insights into
what it takes to achieve LEADERSHIP SUCCESS)

JOB SATISFACTION

The best way to appreciate your job is to imagine yourself without one. Unknown Source

Find a job you love to do and you'll never have to work a day in your life. Unknown Source

No job is so simple that it cannot be done wrong.
Unknown Source

If you love your work, you're likely to be its master; if you hate it, it's likely to be your master. Unknown Source

Don't watch the clock. Do what it does. Keep moving. Sam Levenson

It is a mark of intelligence, no matter what you are doing, to have a good time doing it. Unknown Source

In a University of Minnesota study, 100 people were asked a number of questions:

- "If you were financially independent, would you still want to work? 70% responded YES."
- "Would you want to keep your present job? 70% responded NO."
- "What would you like to do? 70% said a job helping people."
  (Note: How would you respond to these questions? What is your ideal job?)

The real secret of job satisfaction is not in doing what one likes to do, but in liking what one has to do. Unknown Source

The best way to get relief from a monotonous task is to think of ways to improve it. Unknown Source

I try to take just one day at a time....but lately several days have attacked me at once. Unknown Source

If you work for a company, then work for that company with all your might. When the time comes that you can no longer work for the company, regardless of the reason, then make a career decision, but don't hang back and gripe. Unknown Source

Success is to be measured not so much by the position that one has reached in life as by the obstacles that one has overcome while trying to succeed. Unknown Source

What the world needs is more people who will apply to their jobs the same enthusiasm for getting ahead as they display in traffic. Unknown Source

People may forget how fast you did a job, but they will remember how well you did it. Unknown Source

The biggest mistake you can make is to believe you are working for someone else. Unknown Source

I don't care what you do for a living. If you love it, you are a success. Unknown Source

SPIZZERINCTUM is a great believer in *job satisfaction*, but you know something, I find that the harder I work, the more I have of it. SPIZZERINCTUM

CHAPTER TEN

Spizzerinctum Speaks Out! Handling Change And Conflict

Change & conflict have eternal life. They are eternal twins that are ever present in your molecule. They are everywhere and are two of the few constants in your life. They are "here to stay."

As you carry out the daily responsibilities of your job, you experience in various ways the continuing shifts, transitions, and restructuring that occur in the work place—**change.** As you work with the people in your molecule, you experience their opposing needs, drives, wishes, and hostilities—**conflict.** Your leadership success depends on how effective you are in coping with these eternal twins of your molecular life. Let's look at both and see what we can learn.

CHANGE

I am *not* going to try to enumerate the many things that are changing in the "beautiful world of work" that may or may not effect you directly; the list would be too long. However, suffice it to say, organizations of all types are restructuring, being acquired, merging, downsizing, failing, declaring bankruptcy, etc. These are the types of changes that often affect you and the people with whom you work in your molecule. If you ever hope to experience leadership success, you must internalize the fact that change is here to stay and the only thing you can count on to go away is the way things were.

How do you deal with change? Do you resist it? Do you try to ignore it? Do you look for someone to blame for it? Does it make you angry? Do you permit it to take away your job satisfaction or, do you take charge of it and go about solving it with a positive attitude and the cooperation of others?

The biggest myth about change is that we should somehow be *at war* with it, that we should treat it as the enemy to be defeated at all cost in order to maintain stability.

More often than not, change is positive instead of negative. By focusing on the potential positive outcomes, you are more likely to make meaningful progress and less likely to make yourself vulnerable to physical and emotional problems.

It has been uniquely stated that the most effective way to deal with change is to change. Using your power of choice, you can readjust your thinking by responding with a positive attitude and appropriate problem-solving actions.

Dr. Perry W. Buffington said, "Most of the problems associated with change stem from fear and inability to develop a plan of attack. We get so caught up in life changes that it becomes very difficult to view the circumstances objectively. Because we do not know what will happen to us, we tend to blow situations out of proportion. The more negative your thinking concerning upcoming and /or unseen changes, the greater the probability of not adjusting well to change. If you are anticipating a change, get the facts straight. Become familiar with the problem, and never lose sight of your goals. The bottom line is that change is not all bad, but it is inevitable, and one of the few constants in daily living."

Just as your life is a continual process, so it is with change. To effectively handle it, you must be willing to choose behaviors that will facilitate your leadership success. Consider the behaviors below:

- Choose to allow your SPIZZERINCTUM to work for you. With vim, vigor, vitality, and "the will to succeed," you can choose to handle change in positive manner.
- Choose to accept that there are no normal or abnormal ways of dealing with change.
- Choose to exercise patience.
- Choose to have an abiding trust in your own abilities and the abilities of those in your Molecule,
- Choose to understand that dealing with change is not primarily technical, but rather attitudinal.
- Choose to accept the reality that while it may be difficult to let go of the way things are, letting go is most often necessary.
- Choose to accept that successfully dealing with change requires that you must see it not in the context of displacement and disorder, but as an opportunity for progress.
- Choose to understand and accept that dealing with change means being willing to constantly redefine your thinking and actions.
- Finally, choose to internalize the fact that change is not a "once-in-a-lifetime-glad-its-over" happening, but rather it is a constant companion, ever-present in your molecule that you must learn to accept, live with, and handle with attitudes and behaviors of your choice.

CONFLICT

To effectively handle *conflict*, the eternal twin of *change*, you must internalize the fact that conflict, too, is "here to stay." Indeed, conflict literally pervades your daily life. It began with your early childhood behavior when you did not get your way and it will continue throughout your adolescent and adult life as you perceive that somebody has negatively affected something you care about.

Regardless of the conflict situations that touch your molecular life, the most important issue is how you deal with *conflict*. Do you become regularly irritated and defensive? Do you feel the necessity to retaliate? Do you make excuses for your actions and look for someone to blame or, do you first look on the positive side by thinking that this conflict may help solve some of the existing problems in your molecule and then proceed to gather the facts and begin to solve the problem?

As with the handling of change, you must make choices in dealing with conflict. One choice of behavior you will make each time you deal with a specific conflict is that of taking a position. Yes, you will choose positions and behaviors to "stake out" your feelings and beliefs concerning the conflict with which you are dealing. I am presenting the following examples of positions and behaviors with the hope that you will seriously consider them and become consciously aware of them as you deal with conflict in your molecule. Please note, depending on the circumstances and facts involved, these positions and behaviors *may* or *may not* be effective positions for specific conflicts.

- Sometimes the position of "not taking a position" is chosen. In so doing, you have chosen to "duck" or "avoid" becoming involved. For whatever reasons, you believe the conflict is not worth your efforts, i.e., there appears to be no chance of making progress toward your goal.

- Sometimes the position of "adapting" is chosen. When you adapt, your behavior is that of trying to accommodate the position taken by others in order to resolve the conflict and maintains good relations in the Molecule.

- Sometimes the position of "contesting" is chosen. When you contest, your behavior is that of battling to defend your beliefs and feelings about the issues involved

- Sometimes the position of "conceding" is chosen. When you concede, your behavior is that of being willing to settle for a middle ground, i.e., you give up something in order to maintain something you care about.

- Sometime the position of "cooperating" is chosen. When you choose this position, your behavior is that of being cooperative with the goal of arriving at a solution that will satisfy the concerns of all those involved in the conflict. This is often an appropriate position to take in handling conflict.

As stated previously, I hope you will choose to add these conflict-handling positions and behaviors to the programs in your computer (mind) so that you may utilize them the next time conflict makes a visit in your molecule.

Effectively handling *change* and *conflict* is another essential of leadership success. I wish you the best as you seek to cope with these eternal twins that are ever present in your molecule. SPIZZERINCTUM

SPIZZERINCTUMS

(Wise sayings that will give YOU insights into what it takes to achieve LEADERSHIP SUCCESS)

CONFLICT/CHANGE

Nature arranges it so that we can't shut our ears but that we can shut our mouths. Unknown Source

Lord, when we are wrong make us willing to change. And when we are right, make us easy to live with. Peter Marshall

Tempers get you in trouble. Pride keeps you there. Unknown Source

A long dispute means that both parties are wrong. Unknown Source

The next best thing to solving a problem is finding some humor in it. Unknown Source

The best way to forget your own problems is to help others solve theirs. Unknown Source

If you are having trouble with someone in your molecule, try to get to know that person better—you may discover you have something in common. Unknown Source

Any change, even for the better, is always accompanied by drawbacks and discomforts. Unknown Source

When you are through changing you are through. Unknown Source

When you blame others, you give up your power to change. Dr. Robert Anthony

Some leaders change jobs, mates, and friends but never think of changing themselves. Unknown Source

There is nothing wrong with disagreement when the people in your Molecule discuss substantive issues. However, you should first insist on rules of fair play and a focus on the issues rather than the personalities involved. SPIZZERINCTUM

What makes for your leadership success is not the absence of conflict and change in your molecule. It is how you *handle* these "eternal twins". SPIZZERINCTUM

Don't be a conflict/change AVOIDER. Rather, create a climate in your molecule that its okay to try things and fail, to disagree without becoming disagreeable, to make a mistake in one's effort to do a good job. Unknown Source

At times, *change* and *conflict* may be *barriers*, but they may well be *bridges* if you call on your SPIZZERINCTUM. SPIZZERINCTUM

Chapter Eleven

Spizzerinctum Speaks Out!
Positive Leadership Behavior

I have decided to conclude **SPEAKING OUT ON LEADERSHIP SUC-CESS** by sharing one final essential: positive leadership behavior. Your choice of behaviors will play a most important role in determining whether or not you achieve leadership success.

I have said or inferred repeatedly throughout this book:

- Your **leadership** is your **influence**;
- Your **influence** is the **behavior** (s) you choose to exert as you carry out specific actions and plans;
- Your **behavior** (s) determines your **relationships** with the people in your molecule;
- **Leadership** is all about **relationships.**

So clearly, your behavioral choices will determine your relationships with the people with whom you work. *Your leadership success is all about your effective human relationships.*

LEADERSHIP
CHARACTERISTICS AND BEHAVIORS

Each leadership characteristic below will be followed by an example of an overall *positive* and *negative* leadership behavior. After reading each pair of statements, mark the statement that best represents your behavior as you deal with the people in your molecule. Please note that the characteristics and behaviors presented are by no means a complete list. The ones I am sharing emphasize important leadership behaviors that involve relationships with people.

PEOPLE-ORIENTED

____ "I put people first and things second. I enjoy meeting new people. I value relationships. I am happy for others when they succeed. In fact, I enjoy helping others succeed."

____ "I had much rather do my job without becoming overly involved with people. To me having to deal with people is too taxing and too time-consuming. I enjoy my job, but the people I work with often make it unpleasant."

CARING

____ "I care about others' feelings and make it a point to show my concern. I do not put them down when they make a mistake."

____ "I care about others' feelings, but I make it a point not to become overly concerned when they are having one of their 'pity parties' because of one of their 'goof-ups.' I do not hesitate to let them know what I think when things go wrong."

DETERMINATION

___ "I've got SPIZZERINCTUM! Ole Spizz is my *will* (*determination*) to succeed, especially in the positive-relationships-with-other-people-part of my job."

___ "I've got SPIZZERINCTUM, too! Ole Spizz is also my *will* (*determination*) to succeed, especially in that part of my job responsibilities that says I'm responsible to see that they're suppose do their jobs. I'm not too concerned with all that *positive relationship stuff.*"

TRUST

___ "I am honest and trustworthy. My values govern my behaviors and I exhibit those behaviors that help me influence others to the extent that they feel I have their best interest at heart."

___ "I am honest and trustworthy. My values govern my behaviors, but I don't waste a lot of time trying to cater to the *whims* and *feelings* of people. I'm too busy trying to doing the job they are paying me to do."

COMPETENTENCE

___ "I know what I'm doing, know what I'm talking about, and know how to apply my knowledge. If not, I lose my influence with the people with whom I work."

___ "I know what I'm doing and what I'm talking about. I'm very good at my job. In fact, I do my work better than anybody else. If everybody did as well as I, our company would be a lot better off."

RESPONSIBILITY/ACCOUNTABILITY

___ "I hold myself fully responsible and accountable for every thing that happens in my Molecule. I do not blame others or make excuses when things don't go well."

___ "I am a very responsible person and hold myself accountable for the things I do, but I do not hesitate to let other people know, in no uncertain terms, when they mess-up. If I don't they will continue their shoddy ways."

ETHICAL

___ "In my dealings with people, I act in accordance with what is right and wrong consistent with the Golden Rule, the Ten Commandments, and the Laws of the Land."

___ "I consider myself an ethical person, but most of the people I work with don't know the difference between right and wrong. Sometimes I have to get them straightened out."

OPTIMISTIC

___ "I am a positive thinker with a "can do" attitude. I view change and conflict in my Molecule as opportunities to make progress. I do not quickly judge others when they make mistakes, but give them the benefit of the doubt."

___ "I try to be positive and think I am most of the time, but it's hard to work with the people in my department. If I give them the benefit of the doubt they will take advantage of the situation and this will surely lead to even more conflict and more change."

SUPPORTIVE

____ "I help to create an environment in my Molecule that encourages mutual support. Some people have complimented my supportive attitude; I like to help others. I've learned that if you give support you will receive support in return."

____ "I like to do my work and let others do likewise. It just works better that way."

CONSISTENT

____ "I am consistent in the ways I act and think because I believe others should be able to predict my behavior in a given situation. To do otherwise would cause them to be reluctant and throw them off balance and that would hurt our working relationships."

____ "I think I am consistent. However, I don't worry too much about what others think. I like to keep them guessing. If they know how I will react in most situations, they will try to manipulate me."

PERSISTENT

____ "I don't give up easily. I continue to pursue my goals even in the face of difficulties and opposition; however, I am not dogmatic in my persistence because sometimes others may have a better solution."

____ "I am really persistent when it comes to getting my job done. Nothing is more important to me and don't let t other people keep me from doing it my way either."

DEPENDABLE

____ "If I say I will do something, you can count on me to follow through and do it. If something prevents me from getting it done, I will immediately discuss the situation with my boss."

____ "If I say I will do a particular thing and something prevents me from doing it, I'll get to you as soon as I can, but I'm not going to drop everything and run right over. I'm busy and you should understand that my work comes first."

DECISION MAKING

____ "My decisions are always made in the best interest of my organization—not my own self-interest. This causes others to respect my decisions making."

____ "In my opinion, I make good decisions within the framework of my responsibilities. Nobody has complained to me about my decision-making abilities. They better not either."

COMMUNICATIONS

____ "I make every effort to listen to what others have to say and to communicate clearly both orally and in writing."

____ "I don't waste a lot of my valuable time listening to others. I communicate the best I can both orally and in writing. If that's not sufficient, I'm sorry—get someone else to do the job.

OPEN-MINDED

___ "I do not have to always be right. I encourage and accept ideas and suggestions from others. I learn a lot from them that is very helpful."

___ "No one can be right all the time, but I take great pride in being right most of the time. In fact, I'm so well known for being right that I hardly ever receive ideas and suggestions from others."

You have just reviewed fifteen leadership characteristics and a like number of examples of positive and negative behaviors. You probably noticed that the positive examples were *very positive* while the negative examples were *very negative*. I purposely presented the behaviors in this manner in order to make it difficult for you to choose negative behaviors. Why? Because I wanted you to become more consciously aware of how good it feels to identify yourself with positive, people-oriented behaviors that will influence others rather than turn them off. Additionally, I wanted to help you get yourself on the right "behavioral road" that leads directly into the "beautiful world of leadership success."

If you did not identify yourself with at least thirteen of the positive behaviors, you should consider making some changes in your behavioral choices. Negative, non-people behaviors will not lead to leadership success, especially those behaviors that cause others to view you as being an "insensitive person."

Please keep in mind that you do not have to be brilliant or possess a certain combinations of these characteristics and behaviors in order to achieve leadership success. However, you do have to understand that your leadership, in its basic function, is your influence of people. Further, you must understand and accept the fact that the behaviors you exhibit are the result of your choices and that it is your responsibility to choose behaviors that will influence others in such a manner as to help you achieve leadership success.

Sadly, I believe there are a large number of leaders in this world who are, and will remain, ineffective. The reason I believe this is that they never quite get around to understanding and appreciating the needs and feelings of the people with whom they work and socialize. If you are to achieve leadership success, it is essential that you become sensitive to the needs and feelings of those people who populate your molecule and that you exhibit appropriate leadership behaviors.

The essential question is: How can you achieve and maintain a life of leadership success? The answer is simple—**make choices to exhibit positive behaviors and choose to stop using those that are counter-productive.** Once your choices are made, your **SPIZZERINCTUM** will spring into action and work with vim, vigor, vitality, and energy to help you achieve the success desired.

One more important aspect of leadership success I would like for you to consider is SELF-ESTEEM. Take a close look at Virginia Satir's self-esteem essay and the two self-esteem behaviors that follow. Keep in mind that your self-esteem is the image you have of yourself and consists of the thoughts and feelings you have about yourself.

My Declaration of Self-Esteem

I AM ME.

In all the world, there is no one else exactly like me.
There are persons who have some parts like me,
but no one adds up exactly like me.
Therefore, everything that comes
out of me is authentically mine
because I alone chose it.

I own everything about me:
my body, including everything it does;
my mind, including all its thoughts and ideas;

my eyes, including the images of all they behold;
my feeling, whatever they may be—anger, joy,
frustration, love, disappointment, excitement;
my mouth, and all the words that come out of it,
polite, sweet or rough, correct or incorrect;
my voice, loud or soft, and all my actions,
whether they be to others or to myself.

I own my fantasies, my dreams, my hopes my fears.
I own all my triumphs and successes,
all my failures and mistakes.
Because I own all of me, I can become
intimately acquainted with me.
By so doing I can love me and be friendly
with me, in all my parts.
I can then make it possible for all of me to work
in my best interests, aspects about myself that
puzzle me, and other aspects that I do not know.
But as long as I am friendly and loving to myself,
I can courageously and hopefully look for the solutions
to the puzzles and for ways to find out more about me.

However, I look and sound, whatever I say and do, and
whatever I think and feel at a given moment in time is me.
This is authentic and represents where
I am at that moment in time.
When I review later how I looked and sounded,
what I said and did, and how I thought and felt,
some parts may turn out to be unfitting.
I can discard that which is unfitting, and keep that
which proved fitting, and invent something
new for that which I discarded.

I can see, hear, feel, think, say, and do.
I have the tools to survive, and to be close to others,
to be productive, and to make sense and order out
of the world of people and things outside of me.
And, therefore I can engineer me.
I AM ME AND I AM OK.

Virginia Satir

HIGH SELF-ESTEEM

____ I have learned to have positive feelings about myself no matter what happens. I realize that I am a unique person and am proud to be me. I am not easily hurt by criticism; in fact, I accept constructive criticism. I know and accept my strengths and weaknesses. I am able to laugh at (and learn from) my mistakes. I enjoy making friends and having good working relations.

____ I often feel ineffective, worthless, unloved, and lonesome. I am easily hurt by criticism and have an unhappy personal life.

It seems that I have far more failures than successes in my dealings with people. I fear close relationships. I tend to blame my mistakes on others. I am shy but sometimes I become overly aggressive. I find it difficult to make changes and avoid new experiences when possible.

Which one did you choose? High self-esteem? Low self-esteem? Your feelings about YOU will play a big role in your choices of behavior. Choose wisely.

I hope you have profited from my brief discussion of self-esteem, leadership characteristics, and behaviors. I believe you will agree that the positive and negative feelings you have about yourself play a large role in the behaviors you choose to exhibit and that your behaviors influence those people in your molecule either positively or negatively.

My advice: Feel good about yourself; choose positive behaviors; it's worth the effort. SPIZZERINCTUM

SPIZZERINCTUMS

(Wise sayings that will give YOU insights into
what it takes to achieve leadership success)

BEHAVIORS

People are okay; however, their behavior is not always okay . Sonja Beach

People who are unable to build solid, lasting relationships will soon discover that they are unable to leadership success. Unknown Source

I once told a colleague, "You don't get quality and productivity by intimidating and humiliating somebody." He said, "Damn, those are the things I was good at." Unknown Source

Leadership success can be attained if you care more than others think is wise; risk more that others think is safe; dream more than others think is practical; and, expect more than others think is possible. Unknown Source

Those who understand the importance of good human relationships and who are willing to initiate repairs when necessary have a career advantage. Unknown Source

Someday I hope to enjoy enough of what the world calls success so that someone will ask me, "What's the secret of it?" I shall simply say this: "I get up when I fall down." Paul Harvey

Do unto others as you would have them do unto you. Matthew 7: 12

Criticism, like rain, should be gentle enough to nourish one's growth without destroying one's roots. Unknown Source

If a thing goes without saying, then let it. Unknown Source

If you're going to give someone a piece of your mind, make sure you can spare it. Unknown Source

Temper gets you into trouble, pride keeps you there. Unknown Source

Your temper is one of your more valuable possessions, *don't lose it*! Unknown Source

Be wiser than other people are, if you can but do not tell them. Lord Chesterfield

The best way to forget your own problems is to help others solve theirs. Unknown Source

Half the worry in the world is caused by people trying to make decisions before they have sufficient knowledge on which to base a decision. Unknown Source

The real art of conversation is not only to say the right things in the right place but to leave unsaid the wrong things at the tempting moment. Dorothy Nevell

The only people with whom you should try to get even are those who have helped you. Unknown Source

An effective leader is one who can step on toes without messing up the shine. Unknown Source

If there's a single secret to getting along as a leader, it's the same one that insures survival on a snake farm: "KEEP MOVING BUT DON'T MAKE SUDDEN JERK MOVES." Bill Oncken, Jr.

Be willing to share the limelight. After all the successes of those in your molecule are your successes too. Spizzerinctum

The Lord gave us two ends—one to sit on and the other to think with. Success depends on which one we use the most. Unknown Source

You can get anything you want if you help others get what they want. All teamwork is—is liking people and caring enough about them to help them. Your don't have to like everything they do. Unknown Source

If you are patient in a moment of anger, you will escape a hundred days of sorrow. Chinese Proverb

You make more friends in two months by becoming really interested in other people than you can in two years trying to get other people interested in you. Dale Carnegie

If it weren't for the last minute, very little would get done. Unknown Source

General Eisenhower use to demonstrate leadership with a simple piece of string. He'd put it on a table and say: "Pull it and it'll follow you wherever you wish. Push it and it will go nowhere at all." General Dwight Eisenhower

My grandfather once told me that there are two kinds of people; those who do the work and those who take the credit. He told me to try to be in the first group; there was less competition there. Indira Gandhi

Before deciding that some people don't have it, answer the question, "Have they ever been in a position where they could show it?" Unknown Source

Thinking is the hardest work there is, which is probably the reason why so few engage in it. Unknown Source

The difference between a successful career and a mediocre one sometimes consists of leaving about four or five things a day left unsaid. Unknown Source

Rather than enjoying doing something, leaders must enjoy seeing it done. There must be a letting go of hands-on control. Unknown Source

Don't underestimate the strength of a team. It is true—all of us together are smarter than any of us alone. Unknown Source

The next best thing to solving a problem is finding some humor in it. Unknown Source

The behaviors you choose to demonstrate or not demonstrate determine your LEADERSHIP SUCCESS. Unknown Source

Leadership is the exact opposite of ramming orders down the throat of those in your molecule; they do not need to be goaded, prodded, threatened, or reprimanded. Leadership is inspiring others to do their jobs with a since of pride and fulfillment. Spizzerinctum

Successful leaders know that they get the best efforts out of people by working with them....by helping them to do their best. Unknown Source

Leadership requires faith that the people in your molecule will try to do their best. If some of them don't seem to be trying hard enough, the smartest thing to do is to find out the reasons and then try to help them overcome whatever it is that's preventing them from doing their best. Unknown Source

The easiest way to get into leadership trouble is to be right at the wrong time. Unknown Source

You can often tell more about a leader by the way he (she) handles problem than by the way he (she) handles successes. Leith Anderson

If I accept you as you are, I will make you worse; however, if I treat you as though you are what you are capable of becoming, I help you become that. Wolfgang Von Goethe

The key to whatever success I enjoy today is: Don't ask. DO! Vikki Carr

Minds are like parachutes, they only function when open. Unknown Source

The most important leadership behavior is not police duty but problem solving. The most important question is not who is responsible for mistakes but how do we get solutions for the problems before us. Unknown Source

Cooperation is doing with a smile what you have to do anyhow. Unknown Source

Don't try to keep secrets. Communicate, Communicate, Communicate. Problems are caused by people who don't know. Unknown Source

Don't become irrevocably committed to any single solution. There are many paths to the top of the hill. Unknown Source

Leaders must learn not to over-analyze the past when they are confronted with failure. They must quickly understand what went wrong, accept responsibility for their part in the failure, and then move on. Unknown Source

When you are wrong, admit it. Almost everyone will know it anyway. Your capitulation will be seen as reasonableness. Unknown Source

If the actions of your behavior ever takes *responsibility* away from those with whom you work, then you have dehumanized them. SPIZZERINCTUM

There is no market for gloom and doom behavior. You cannot sell it. What the world wants, needs, and will buy is positive behaviors like cheerfulness, smiling, forgiveness, patience, love, praise, honesty, morality, thank you, please, and I'm sorry. Unknown Source

Leadership is also a performing art—a collection of practices and behaviors—not a position. Kouze & Posner

Every failure is a dress rehearsal for success. Herbert Harris

You become what you think of most of the time. Earle Nightingale

Whether you are able to develop positive, gratifying, and empowering relationships to a large extent determines whether and to what degree you will achieve your goals and realize your vision. Herbert Harris

All human beings have their weaknesses, but not all of us realize them, come to grips with them, or offset their negative impact—leaders must accomplish the paradoxical task of managing their darker sides. Donald T. Phillips

The behavior of *procrastination* is a close relative of incompetence and a handmaiden of inefficiency. Unknown Source

Oh Lord, let my words today be sweet and tender for tomorrow I may have to eat them. Unknown Source

CHAPTER TWELVE

Spizzerinctum Speaks Out! Hopes I Have For You And Your Leadership Success

Congratulations!! You have reached the final chapter. Here are my **Hopes** to help summarize for you the leadership concepts, principles, and ideas that I have shared. As you read them, please remember this wise saying of Napoleon Bonaparte:

"A leader is a dealer of hope."

- I sincerely hope that you will internalize the fundamental meaning of leadership, which is nothing more or less than your influence. You were born with an influence; therefore, you were born a leader—certainly not an effective leader because there is a lot that can and should be learned about this aspect of your existence.

- I hope these words become "programs in your computer" (your mind), and that you will draw on their meanings and implications to help you experience leadership success:

LEADERSHIP   SPIZZERINCTUM   MOLECULE
CHOICE   ATTITUDE   CHANGE   CONFLICT
PRAISE   EXPECTIONS   JOB SATISFACTION

- I hope you will internalize the fact that you were born with the power of choice and that your choices dictate your behaviors. In turn, your behaviors determine your successes and failures for the rest of your life, including your success as the President of your Molecule Of Leadership.

- I hope when you make your next mistake (hopefully not too serious) that you are big enough to take full responsibility without casting blame or making excuses. Don't ever forget these sayings:

> **"A man/woman is never a failure**
> **until he/she blames someone else."**
>
> **"An excuse is a tool of incompetence**
> **built on monuments of nothingness**
> **and those who specialize in them**
> **are seldom good for anything else."**

- I hope you never forget that "you cannot manage people; they are unmanageable." You lead people with the power of your influence."

- I hope the three components of your leadership, your Competence, Personality, Character will work positively for you as you choose behaviors that will cultivate the support of the people in your Molecule.

- I hope you will never forget that trust is the cornerstone of effective relationships and that it is your responsibility to deal with people is such a manner that they will trust you. (Remember, if they don't trust you, it is your fault.)

- I hope you never forget that "no person is an island." You get your job done with the active support of the people in your molecule; therefore, as President of your Leadership Molecule, your most important responsibility is to cultivate the support of the people with whom you work.

- I hope you will be continually aware that people are okay but their behavior may not always be okay. (Choose not to take things too personally!)

- I hope you internalize that you can get *almost* anything you want if you help others get what they want. Working together really works.

- I hope you never forget the value of your attitude as it relates to your leadership success. Your attitude is either positive or negative. It will either greatly help your relationships or greatly hinder your relationships. Attitude is a choice—*your* choice.

- I hope you will never forget the response of the third ditch-digger: "Mister, I am helping to build a cathedral." Helping to build a better department/organization/unit is behavior that will not go unnoticed.

- I hope you will always remember that "life is 10% of what happens to you and 90% of how you react to it." Make it a habit to react positively and you will soon learn that a positive reaction beats a negative reaction every time.

- I hope you maintain a conscious awareness that change & conflict have eternal life and that these eternal twins are ever present in your molecule—and everybody else's too. It is your responsibility to choose behaviors that result in positive solutions.

- I hope these words from "The Station" will ring in your mind for a long time: "Sooner or later, we must realize there is no station, no one place to arrive once and for all. The true joy of life is the trip. The station is only a dream. It constantly out distances us."

- I hope you remember the value of praise and that praise is a power of your choice. One of the basic needs of everyone in your molecule is to feel important, to feel that their efforts contribute to the organization, and to feel good about who they are. It is your responsibility to make them feel important by offering a word of praise when it is deserved.

- I hope you will be daily aware that high expectations lead to high performance, while low expectations lead to low performance. The people in your molecule, including you, most often become/achieve what is expected of them. There is power in your expectations.

- I hope you never forget this basic truth from "The Story Of The Wise Man": Whether the dove the Prince held in his hand was alive or dead depended upon the Prince and what he did with what he had. The same is true for the dove that you hold in your hands, i.e., the ideas, concepts and principles I have shared with you. What will you do with them? Will they live to flourish and help you achieve leadership success or will they die from lack of thought and utilization, thus, making no contributing to your leadership success? It depends on you and what you do with what **SPIZZERINCTUM** has shared.

- I hope you realize that your leadership success is impossible unless you have a high degree of job satisfaction. Remember that job satisfaction is a choice. Make the right choice!

- I hope you will constantly remember that the behaviors you exhibit as you work with the people in your molecule are actions of your choice. These actions become your influence—your leadership. So *"behavior"* yourself in a positive, helpful manner and leadership success *"will follow you all the days of your life"*.

• "Of all the forces that make for a better world, none is so indispensable, none so powerful, as HOPE. Without HOPE people are only half alive. With HOPE they dream and think and work." Charles Sawyer

My final hope is that you will internalize the summary statements that follow:

• Your LEADERSHIP SUCCESS is dependent on the success of your RELATIONSHIPS with those people in your Molecule.

• Your RELATIONSHIPS SUCCESS is dependent upon the BEHAVIORS you choose to exhibit as you work with people.

• The BEHAVIORS you choose to exhibit are behaviors of your INFLUENCE. These behaviors are either positive or negative.

• Your INFLUENCE is your LEADERSHIP. Your LEADERSHIP is your INFLUENCE.

• You were born a LEADER because you were born with and INFLUENCE. However, your LEADERSHIP SUCCESS is ultimately dependent upon your POWER OF CHOICE and your SPIZZERINCTUM.

Dear Reader:

I hope you will never forget that I am your SPIZZERINCTUM, your "will to succeed," and that I reside deep inside your very soul to help you achieve leadership success. The moment you make a choice to succeed in any endeavor, I spring into action, acting vigorously and with determination, to help you succeed.

It has been a *pure pleasure* and *perfect delight* to share with you by SPEAKING OUT ON LEADERSHIP SUCCESS. Don't forget I'm inside you, awaiting your choices that summons my spizzerinctumly actions.

In the meantime, so long Saddle Pal—Keep it downhill and shady, pardner!

Most Sincerely,
SPIZZERINCTUM

Appendix A

SPIZZERINCTUM JARGON

I want all of you to know that this JARGON idea was not mine. Even so, I rather like it; I think it's rather cute. This all got started several years ago when Ron Butler shared the word SPIZZERINCTUM with Dr. Louis Schmier, teacher-professor of history at Valdosta State University, Valdosta, Georgia. Dr. Schmier became so intrigued with me and what I meant that he created a jargon so that he and Ron could continue their email correspondence in a *profound* fashion. Ha! Thank you, Dr. Schmier, for your JARGON about me that shows my far-reaching breadth and depth. Now, Dear Leader, go ahead and enjoy the SPIZZERINCTUM JARGON.

SPIZZERINCTUMER: A practitioner of spizzerinctum.

SPIZZERINCTUMIST: A philosophy of spizzerinctum

SPIZZERINCTUMOSOPHY: The philosophy of spizzerinctum

SPIZZERINCTUMIZE: To subject to spizzerinctum

SPIZZERINCTUMISTIC: Having a spizzerinctum out look

SPIZZERINCTUMODE: A mood of being in spizzerinctum

SPIZZERINCTUMNESS: A condition of spizzerinctum

SPIZZERINCTUMLY: A condition of being influenced by spizzerinctum

SPIZZERINCTUMILE: Having a quality of spizzerinctum

SPIZZERINCTUMIDE: Having the physical characteristics of spizzerinctum

SPIZZERINCTUMIZER: One who implements spizzerinctum

SPIZZERINCTUMIZATION: Results of spizzerinctum

SPIZZERINCTUMDOX: Pure spizzerinctum

SPIZZERINCTUMITIC: Marked by spizzerinctum

SPIZZERINCTUMITY: Minute amounts of spizzerinctum

SPIZZERINCTUMIVE: Lastingly spizzerinctum

SPIZZERINCTUMITIS: Excessive spizzerinctum

SPIZZERINCTUMOID: Having the physical shape of spizzerinctum

SPIZZERINCTUMULAR: Resembling or related to spizzerinctum

SPIZZERINCTUMOME: A mass gathering of spizzerinctum followers

SPIZZERINCTUMISTICLY: An action influenced by spizzerinctum

SPIZZERINCTUMOLOGY: The study of spizzerinctum

SPIZZERINCTUMOLOGIST: An expert on the study of spizzerinctum

SPIZZERINCTUMTUMGY: A celebration of spizzerinctumers, spizzerinctumists, and spizzerinctumologists

SPIZZERECTUM: The low ebb or terminal state of one's Spizzerinctum.

(Note: This is the only spizzerinctum term that was not created by Dr. Schmier. This one came from friend, Betty Lewis, who replied when Ron asked her how her Spizzerinctum was today, "It's not spizzerinctum today, Ron, it's more like Spizzerectum." Thus, the final term of the Spizzerinctum Jargon.)

Appendix B

MORE SPIZZERINCTUMS

(Wise sayings that will give YOU insights into
what it takes to achieve LEADERSHIP SUCCESS)

"DON'T EVER GIVE UP!" Down through the ages, many people in many different situations have uttered these words as their "will to succeed" came under intense pressure "to give up and walk away." I am repeating these words again with the hope that you will choose to call on your SPIZZERINCTUM in order to achieve over and over again your LEADERSHIP SUCCESS. The statements that follow will help you see the value of this exhortation: "DON'T EVER GIVE UP!"

Henry Ford failed and went broke five times before he finally succeeded.

Franklin Roosevelt was struck down by polio, but never quit.

It took Noah Webster 36 years to compile Webster's Dictionary.

Abraham Lincoln failed in business, lost numerous elections, had a nervous breakdown, but never quit.

Ernest Hemingway is said to have revised THE OLD MAN manuscript 80 times before submitting it for publication.

Edison failed in over 3,000 attempts to make the light bulb work. (When asked by a reporter why he failed over 3,000 times, Edison looked at the reporter and said, "FAILED! I have never failed. What I have done is successfully identify 3,000 ways which will not work.")

You will be knocked down, but you have to keep getting up…and up…and up…and up.

With the grip of determination this frog has, as evidenced by the look on the birds face, do you think IT will ever give up? Not a chance! May this be akin to your SPIZZERINCTUMOUS grip on Leadership Success!

"IF IT IS TO BE IT IS UP TO ME

If you will internalize this wise saying and just say YES to leadership success, SPIZZERINCTUM will see to it that leadership success say YES to you.

Appendix C

MORE SPIZZERINCTUMS

WISE SAYINGS FROM "THINK"
BY DR. ROBERT ANTHONY

If you are constantly being mistreated, you're cooperating with the treatment.

The angry people are those who are most afraid.

Others can stop you temporarily, only you can do it permanently.

If you worry about what might be, and wonder what might have been, you will ignore what is.

Before you can break out of prison, you must first realize you're locked up.

Whatever you are willing to put up with, is exactly what you will have.

Your interpretation of what you see and hear, is just that, your interpretation.

If you find a good solution and become attached to it, the solution may become your next problem.

Criticize the performance, not the performer.

If you *require* someone to change, you require that person to lie to you.

We fear the thing we want the most. The biggest risk in life is not risking.

Worry comes from the belief you are powerless.

Your ability to relax is in direct proportion to your ability to trust life.

What you are afraid to do is a clear indicator of the next thing you need to do.

If you stick your head in the sand, one thing is for sure, you'll get your rear kicked.

The above quotes come from THINK, a Berkley Book, published by Berkley Publishing Group, 200 Madison Avenue, New York, N.Y. 10016 by arrangement with the author, Dr. Robert Anthony.

APPENDIX D

MORE SPIZZERINCTUMS

(Wise sayings that will give YOU insights into
what it takes to achieve LEADERSHIP SUCCESS)

LESSONS FROM GEESE

As each goose flaps its wings, it creates an "uplift" for the bird following. By flying in a V formation, the whole flock adds 71% flying range than if each bird flew alone.

Lesson: People who share a common direction and sense of community can get where they are going quicker and easier because they are traveling on the thrust of one another.

Whenever a goose falls out of formation, it suddenly feels the drag and resistance of trying to fly alone, and quickly gets back into formation to take advantage of the "lifting power" of the bird immediately in front.

Lesson: If we have as much sense as a goose, we will stay in formation with those who are headed where we want to go.

When the lead goose gets tired, it rotates back into the formation and another goose flies at the point position.

Lesson: It pays to take turns doing the hard tasks and sharing leadership—with people, as with geese, interdependent with each other.

The geese in formation honk from behind to encourage those up front to keep up their speed.

Lesson: We need to make sure our honking from behind is encouraging—not something less than helpful.

When a goose gets sick or wounded or shot down, two geese drop out of formation and follow it down to help and protect him. They stay with the goose until it is either able to fly again or dies. Then they launch out on their own with another formation or catch up with the flock.

Lesson: If we have as much sense as geese, we'll stand by each other like that.

Author Unknown

Appendix E

MORE SPIZZERINCTUMS

(Wise sayings that will give YOU insights into
what it takes to achieve LEADERSHIP SUCCESS)

RELATIONSHIPS

Twelve Lesson Learned From A Lifetime Of Reading Ann Landers

1. You are responsible for your own happiness. No one can make you feel inferior unless you allow them to do it.

2. People won't stay mad at you long if you can say, "I was wrong, and I am truly sorry. I hope you will forgive me."

3. When something is troubling you, tell someone you trust instead of trying to cover it up. You will be surprised to learn that the other person has been through something similar.

4. Don't pass up an opportunity to tell people you care about them. You may never get another chance.

5. Reserve judgment until you know all the facts. Even then, keep your mouth shut if no useful purpose is served by adding your two cents' worth.

6. Be grateful for your good health and the health of those you love. Be aware that without good health, money and success mean little.

7. If you enjoy your work and your life, you are rich. If you aren't happy with either, how can money help.

8. If you are having a rotten day, don't take it out on those around you. Simply say to yourself, "Today is a rotten day. Tomorrow will be better." That attitude will improve your disposition as well as your digestive system.

9. Spend time with your children. It's the best investment you will ever make.

10. Don't be afraid to try something you think you can't do. Nothing ventured, nothing gained

11. There's no such thing as the perfect man or woman. Look for the best overall package of kindness, consideration, ambition and, intelligence. Otherwise, you will spend your life alone.

12. You can respect and learn from people, even if you don't like them. Be aware that you can learn something from every one, because every person in the world knows something you don't know.

    (Contributed by Nancy L. Jacobs, Omaha, Nebraska. Printed in Raleigh News & Observer's Ann Lander's column, August 4, 2000)

Appendix F

MORE SPIZZERINCTUMS

(Wise sayings that will give YOU insights into
what it takes to achieve LEADERSHIP SUCCESS)

SPIZZERINCTUM'S TEN COMMANDMENTS OF
MOLECULAR BEHAVIORS THAT INFLUENCE OTHERS
POSITIVELY AND LEAD TO YOUR LEADERSHIP SUCCESS

1. Thou shall keep your tongue under control, always saying less about others than you think.

2. Thou shall not blame others when things go wrong, realizing that such behavior is entirely counter-productive to your relationships.

3. Thou shall not miss the opportunity to make others feel important by expressing a kind, encouraging, well-deserved *"word of praise"* to let them know that their work/help is valued and appreciated.

4. Thou shall be consciously aware that when it comes to influencing people your attitude is your most priceless possession.

5. Thou shall let the people in your Molecule know that they are important and that their contributions are important.

6. Thou shall not forget that the best away to avoid placing too much emphasis on your own problems is to help others solve theirs.

7. Thou shall never make decisions or draw conclusions before you have sufficient knowledge on which to base a decision.

8. Thou shall try to get even only with those who have helped you.

9. Thou shall always be aware that the easiest way to get into trouble is to be right at the wrong time

10. Thou shall not keep secrets; rather, communicate, communicate, communicate, remembering that most problems are caused by what people don't know.

NOTE: SPIZZERINCTUM'S rock, solid foundation for each of these Ten Commandments is the GOLDEN RULE: "Do unto others as you would have them do unto you." (Note: These commandments are a compilation of "wise sayings" from previous SPIZZERINCTUMS at the end of various chapters where credit, if known, was given.)

REFERENCES

(**Note:** In addition to the references below, acknowledgement and credit to other references appear throughout the book.)

Gilley, Kay. Leading From The Heart. Newton (MA) Battenworth-Heinemann, 1997

Glasser, Dr. William. Reality Therapy. Copyright, 1965 Harper & Row Publishers Inc. New York

Graham, Billy. The Moral Weight Of Leadership. A letter by Billy Graham was printed in New York Times, March 17, 1998

Hand, Keith D. Attitude Is Everything: A Tune-up To Enhance Your Life. (Dubuque, Iowa) Kendall/Hunt Publishing Company. 1995

Helmstetter, Shad. Choices. New York. Pocket Books (Simon & Schuster Inc. 1998

Maxwell, John C. Leadership Quotes: Inspirational Quotes and Insights For Leaders. (Tulsa, OK) 1994

Moore, James W. Attitude Is Your Paintbrush: It Colors Every Situation. Dimensions For Living (Nashville, TN) 1998

Oncken, William, Jr. Managing Management Time: Whose Got The Monkey? (Englewood Cliffs, NJ.) Prentice Hall, Inc. 1984

Oncken, William, Jr. Time Management For Managers and Professionals: Participants Text. Produced jointly by William Oncken Corporation and Deltak, Inc. 1978

Phillip, Donald T. Lincoln On Leadership. New York. Warner Books. 1992

Sandler, Len. Self-Fulfilling Prophency: Better Management By Magic. Article in Training 61 Magazine. February, 1986